Embracing
Our Queenly Anointing

Anointed for such a time as this (Esther 4:14)

Dr. Sharon Smith

Embracing Our Queenly Anointing

ISBN 978-1727389784

Published by Rhema Publishing

Rhemapublishing1@gmail.com

All scripture taken from:

Amplified Version of the Bible and New King James Version

ACKNOWLEDGEMENT

This book is dedicated first to the Lord and then to all my beloved sisters in Christ, whom God has anointed "FOR SUCH A TIME AS THIS". I especially dedicate this book to the Queens I met on my missions trip in August, 2017 to St. Vincent and the Grenadines. I dedicate it to all God's Queens (present and future). Read this book and embrace your anointing as QUEENS.

Special thanks to:
Richard & Angela Gordon: Cover Designer
& Andy Pascal: Photographer

CONTENTS

About the Author

Dr. Sharon Smith was born in Jamaica West Indies. Her relocation to the United States in September 1970 became the turning point in her life. She attended Grace Gospel Chapel in Harlem New York for 17 years, and became a member of Bethel Gospel Assembly also in Harlem in 1987. This is where a life of ministry truly began for Sharon, as she sought to follow the inscription written on the outside wall of that church, "ENTER TO LEARN GO FORTH TO SERVE."

Dr. Sharon is a professional Christian counselor, a professor and an ordained minister. She also facilitates Inspired Wholeness Ministries, a ministry for women, especially those who have been hurt along the way. She holds a Bachelor of Science Degree in Organizational Management, a Master of Science Degree in Counseling from Mercy College, graduating Suma Cum Laude, and a Doctorate in Biblical Counseling/Biblical Studies from Master's International University of Divinity, graduating with honors. She is currently pursuing an Ed.D. at Concordia University. Sharon is the author of *Christian Divorce Wars, Weapons for Victory, The Shepherd's Call, 31 Days of Wholeness and Newbies in the Kingdom*. She is also the editor of a Christian women's magazine called *The Bridge*.

Dr. Sharon is the mother of two adult children; Shanae Nicholas and Jason Smith. She also has a son-in-law Nick, and a daughter-in-law Cabrea; and she is the grandmother of Alex, Leilani and Caleb Nicholas (her pride and joy).

INTRODUCTION

As I lay in my bed one Sunday morning while residing in San Diego, California, for a season, I heard a sound on my phone, alerting me there was a text message. It was 5:00 am California time so I knew it had to be one of my east coast friends whose time zone was 3 hours ahead. I was absolutely correct it was a pastor friend of mine (Dr. Denise Thorpe), in Florida, with an urgent message saying "please call me when you are up, I want to pray with you for a few minutes". As I am always ready to seize the moment to pray I called immediately. She prayed for me with urgency in her spirit and though she did not pray for long she covered all the bases.

Throughout the prayer she emphasized me walking in my Esther anointing, which was something no one had ever prayed so specifically concerning me before. As I got off the phone I went to the book of Esther, got down on my knees and asked the Lord to reveal to me what it would mean for me to embrace this Esther anointing. In the days to come as I read this very familiar book of the Bible, God took me between the lines of the book, helping me to understand and formulate what it meant to be His daughter. It basically meant I had a royal lineage that I had not really tapped into, though I have called myself His daughter for many years. Although He had anointed me for greatness and stretched out His royal scepter giving me orders to walk in my Queenly anointing, I had held back, because in my thoughts I felt unworthy of any type of honor. I decided that memorable Sunday morning in October 2016, to study the book of Esther yet another time, but with a new awakening in my spirit to embrace my anointing as a royal daughter of the King of kings. It is my hope that as my sisters in Christ read this book; they too will recognize their true calling and make the decision that no matter what role they play in this life, they have been given a robe of righteousness to enable them to walk in their royal Queenly anointing.

This book that you are holding has been fleshed out as a result of God's desire to refresh your mind as to what your purpose is as a woman walking in her created calling to be successful victorious and royal . I recognize that many of you have been through things that, at times, seemed so overwhelming you chose to keep them to yourself. However, your loving Father, the King of all kings, who has seen and continues to see the rugged road that you walk, desires that you embrace your royal anointing, knowing that the circumstances of your past and maybe even your present, is a crucial part of your future face to face encounter with your Father the King. Be resolute in allowing Him to use you for such a time as this. I pray healing, restoration, deliverance and blessing on you in this season, as you boldly embrace your **QUEENLY ANOINTING**.

Being Deposed as Queen

Occasionally people are removed from positions so others can replace them. President Richard Nixon was the 37th president of the United States and I recall the circumstances surrounding his impeachment in 1972. The nation referred to that crucial era as the Watergate experience. I am not a political connoisseur, but it doesn't take much political savvy to comprehend the underlying factors leading up to his impeachment. The country wasted no time in immediately replacing him with his vice president Gerald Ford. It would seem that during his reign as vice president Ford had been groomed for the possibility of one day becoming president. While in the role of vice president, he was probably given the opportunity to watch, at times from a distance, what his predecessor was doing right and what he was doing wrong. He, more than likely, wondered what it would be like to be president, and possibly envisioned vying for the position in the future. However, he was given the position on the heels of someone else's indiscretion.

As daughters of the King we too are being groomed for certain positions in the kingdom and at times we even question whether we are worthy. We find ourselves in positions on the job, in the church and even at home that seem to keep us at a distance, or at times in the background peeling the potatoes. We become so entrenched in those positions we never rise to the occasion to be anything more than what we are. The thought of striving to be anything else brings

11

a certain level of fear that cripples us from moving forward. Sometimes in order to get us to move into our position of royalty God has to move others out of the way. In some instances it may be as a result of someone's indiscretion, their demise or just because their time is up, just to open our eyes as to where he wants us to go. He may even allow loved ones to be removed from our lives (i.e. husbands, children, parents) to move us into our royal positions. Some of us have received special anointing from God, but the crippling effects of circumstances have kept us stagnant and unable to move. Paul reminded Timothy, his protégé, to *"fan into flames the gift of God that was given to him from his mother and grandmother through the laying on of hands"* (2 Timothy 1:6). Sometimes as daughters of the King we may wonder how that verse may even apply to us. The gift given to this young man was compared to a fire that he had to fan in order for it to ignite and become a flame.

We have all been given special gifts, but they must be fueled in order to remain strong and this only happens through prayer, faith and obedience, even when all hell is breaking loose in our lives. Though Esther is the queen we aspire to emulate, we must also take a glance at her predecessor Vashti, who in addition to her disobedience to the king exemplified some characteristics befitting a woman of integrity. We tend, at times, to focus on her disobedience to her husband the king, when in fact; this was the catalyst which led to her obedience to her Father the King of kings. I am by no means condoning being disobedient and obstinate with one's husband, however, Vashti must have really had to ponder her action as to whether she wanted to parade (possibly naked), before a bunch of drunken men.

Though the book of Esther gives no real background to the life of Queen Vashti, she enters the scene as the disobedient and unsubmissive wife of King Xerxes (Ahasuerus in Hebrew). Although much is not said about her and the lifestyle she enjoyed, her name, Vashti, which is translated beautiful woman, gives us a glimpse of at least what she looked like. She must have been one of the most beautiful women in the province of Persia, because her husband the King, in his drunken state, sought to boastfully parade her at one of his drinking indulgencies. Although the story of Vashti is only revealed in a few short sentences in the book of Esther, she stands as an intricate part of how the drama unfolds. While the majority of the book surrounds Esther, from our standpoint Queen Vashti is a major character, who was deposed from the palace because she re- fused to be on display for her husband and his drunken cohorts. It seemed her self-respect meant more to her than the high honor of being the wife of a King. Therefore, she chose to disobey his orders at the risk of being replaced as his Queen.

In chapter 1 verse 10-11 the Bible declares; in a drunken state he commanded his eunuchs to *"bring her before him, wearing her royal crown, in order to display her beauty...for she was lovely to look at"*. King Xerxes wanted to show off all his royal possessions, which included his wife. Instead of catering to the narcissism and provocative nature of her husband and his drunkard cronies, she bravely gave up an empire. Instead of lowering her self-worth and her feminine modesty, Vashti acknowledged shame and ultimate deposal. The real leader in that drunken state of affairs was the woman who shunned from public exhibition, even at the king's authority.

Vashti was determined to protect her integrity; and if we, as twenty first century women, fall short in reverencing our life, we will by no means receive the best that God has for us. It is very unfortunate that in our contemporary society we have such a stringent disregard for our sense of worth as it relates to our bodies, in an effort to win favor with men, and join the popularity of those we find most attractive and sensual. Style and fame are an unfortunate cost for the thrashing of our self-worth. Christian principles may seem unfashionable and in disagreement with today's fad, but the favor of God engulfs those who choose the path less walked.

As it relates to the sexual revolution of our time, if we take a look at our teenage and young adult women, we recognize the length and breadth some will take to measure up to the so called "popular" crowd. It seems shameful for some, in what has become the minority, to admit, when confronted by the general public, that they are virgins. I venture to say if we took a poll of the young women in our churches we would find most have bit the proverbial bullet, and submitted to the sensuous allure of some young man, probably in the church. We put ourselves in situations; disregard the way of escape provided by our Father and run the risk of future defamation. When we finally come to our senses we find that we have already been paraded and our integrity sabotaged, all so we can win favor in our worldly empire, and not be dethroned from popularity.

Unlike the modest Queen Vashti of Persia we find ourselves living in a careless age, when integrity and self-worth is no longer fashionable. I recall reading the book of Esther several times and for the most part I focused on the successor, without paying much attention to her predecessor. This least talked about Queen, by choosing to be deposed from the empire, is a representation of the royal daughters in the kingdom of God who choose, what the Bible refers to as *"the small, narrow and difficult to travel path that leads the way to[everlasting] life, because there are few who find it"* (Matthew 7:14 AMP). The fact that few find it speaks to the fact that it is not the most popular road traveled. I believe Vashti knew the cost of her decision, but decided to make the ultimate sacrifice for the sake of

14

her integrity and God allowed this so He could get glory through her successor.

As twenty first century Christian women, we too have a role to play in the royal palace that we refer to as the sophisticated church. However, at times we sacrifice our integrity to remain famous in this earthly kingdom. Sometimes we do things that we realize is totally outside the realm of our character so we can be liked and embraced by the masses. Our Queenly example, Vashti, teaches us by her actions to adhere to the Biblical declaration that *"All things are lawful [that is, morally legitimate, permissible], but not all things are beneficial or advantageous. All things are lawful, but not all things are constructive [to character] and edifying [to spiritual life]"* (1 Corinthians 10:23 AMP).

Therefore, though we are in the church, at times being asked to play many major roles, we must always remember our ultimate allegiance is to our Father the King. What would He say about some of the roles we play? Was this a part of His will and plan or are we playing roles because they feel and sound good? Has He beckoned us to the banqueting table to parade for His glory, or are we caught in ravishes of earthly, or possibly self-glorification?

Sometimes it's difficult to decipher why we dilute our Queenly heritage to the detriment of our future, in an effort to win the recognition of pastors and church leaders. Like Vashti, we have to be resolute in our decisions to secure our eternal heavenly rewards, instead of vying for positions where we only attain temporary rewards on earth. Physical beauty is short-lived but inner beauty is everlasting. Though Vashti must have known she was beautiful to look at, she must also have known and wanted to preserve the inner loveliness that Proverbs 31 speaks of when it says *"Charm and grace are deceptive, and [superficial] beauty is vain, But a woman who fears the LORD [reverently worshiping, obeying, serving, and trusting Him with awe-*

15

filled respect], she shall be praised" (verse 30 AMP). The book of Esther makes no reference to God; however, He is ever present throughout. Vashti's superficial beauty had the power to win her favor with her husband the king and men in general, but instead she chose being deposed over being exposed.

How many of us, when given the choice, would prefer being demoted to being promoted? I venture to say promotion is much easier to embrace, because it makes us feel we have attained positive acknowledgment from the one doing the promoting. On our jobs we work tirelessly to achieve exactly what the boss requires, and when overlooked for promotion or recognition, we drown in the sorrow of wondering why. We tend to forget that real promotion comes from God: *For promotion cometh neither from the east, nor from the west, nor from the south. But God is the judge: he putteth down one, and setteth up another"* (Psalm 75:6-7 KJV). In the narrative in the book of Esther we recognize that it was mandatory for Vashti to be demoted as Queen, in order for Esther to be promoted. However, Vashti's de- motion was also an opportunity for her integrity to be manifested to those watching from a distance. Sometimes in order to be the Queens that God anointed us to be we must suffer demotion to se- cure our integrity. In those demoting seasons we, at times, fight to win promotions that God does not endorse.

In Esther 1:18-19 AMP. The Bible says *"This [very] day the ladies of Persia and Media who have heard of the queen's refusal will speak [in the same way] to all the king's officials, and there will be plenty of contempt and anger. If it pleases the king, let a royal command be issued by him and let it be written in the laws of the Persians and Medes so that it cannot be repealed or modified, that Vashti is no longer to come before King Ahasuerus; and let the king give her royal position to another who is better and more worthy than she".* In essence, this caused public embarrassment for the king and his merry men. Sometimes in our deposed positions we forget that God promised us He had thoughts of peace and not evil about us, and it was in an effort to give us hope and a future (Jeremiah 29:11). Much is not said about where Vashti ended up after her deposal, but I venture to say God had a plan for this heroic Queen who, by losing her earthly royalty, attained a majestic position in His royal economy.

We have to realize that as God's regal daughters we can't be too quick to attain secular accolades, to the detriment of losing what God really has for us. In the Biblical narrative of Hannah, another one of God's noble Queens, we read that she was a wife of Elkanah. However, she had a rival in the form of Peninnah, his other wife, who antagonized her as a result of her apparent barrenness. This bantering went on for years because her opponent realized Hannah was the favored wife. 1 Samuel 1:4-6, announces; *"When the day came that Elkanah sacrificed, he would give portions [of the sacrificial meat] to Peninnah his wife and all her sons and daughters. But to Hannah he would give a double portion, because he loved Hannah, but the LORD had given her no children. Hannah's rival provoked her bitterly, to irritate and embarrass her, because the LORD had left her childless"*.

Sometimes we too come to a place of barrenness in some areas of our lives and suffer ridicule from those who seem to be basking in all the blessings. Hence, we forget the promises of our Father the King to bless us. In essence, we feel deposed, meanwhile God just wants to use, what seems like deposal, to restore our integrity and bless us indeed. In the narrative of Hannah, she resolved to intense prayer. She exclaimed in her prayer *"O LORD of hosts, if you will indeed look on the affliction (suffering) of your maidservant and remember, and not forget your maidservant"* (1 Samuel 1:11). Sometimes during our seasons of displacement we feel like God has forgotten about us. The book of Esther doesn't say anything about Vashti's mind-set as she watched her successor take the reigns as Queen, but I believe in her humanness she probably felt forgotten, and probably had to be reminded that God still knew her name (beautiful woman) and had destiny waiting in the wings.

I beckon to my seemingly displaced sisters today, the ones God has called to destiny, the ones who must walk in their regal positions, the ones who must, through, at times, difficult adversities, embrace their Queenly anointing; don't quit because God has not forgotten your name. You are clay in the Potter's hands being fashioned into royalty. *"I went down to the potter's house, and saw that he was working at the wheel. But the vessel that he was making from clay was spoiled by the potter's hand; so he made it over, reworking it and making it into another pot that seemed good to him"* (Jeremiah 18:3-4).

I venture to say that like Jeremiah, Queen Vashti, after leaving her earthly kingdom, went down to her heavenly Potter's house and there realized what she thought was demotion, was really God reworking her clay formation into something new and fit for His royal palace. As we begin this journey of exploring what God has for us on our royal expedition, I endeavor to say, we too, like Vashti, must reroute to the Potter's house. God, in what may seem at times like horrific circumstances, is fashioning us into the Queenly vessels that He wants to utilize in His kingdom.

How has Vashti's deposal impacted some of your decisions?

****

Notes

Preparing for our Royal Lineage

As women, when it comes to preparing for our wedding day we usually take great pains to look our very best. God equates His Church to that of being a bride and in Ephesians 5:27 He says He wants to *"present her to himself in splendor, without spot or wrinkle or any such thing, that she might be holy and without blemish"*. In September 2016, I attended my godson's wedding at the Justice of the Peace office in Los Angeles, CA. As I walked into the outer courtyard of the office there was a long line of couples waiting to get married. Though a few of the brides looked like they actually took real time to prepare, most were dressed casually, as if it was just another day at the park. Some looked like they just rolled out of bed that morning and said "let's get married". As I drove home from that event I recall thinking how the preparation time for brides has diminished and how little time some take to be adorned, for what is supposed to be one of the most important days of their lives. This speculation is not meant to degrade any of the brides that have chosen to go that route; it is just an observation of how brides have changed when it comes to how much adornment is required to prepare for that special day.

As a result of our Father being the King of all kings there is a level of preparation required for us to get ready for the royal lineage we are afforded. 2 Corinthians 5:17 AMP declares, *"Therefore, if any-*

one is in Christ [that is, grafted in, joined to Him by faith in Him as Savior], he is a new creature [reborn and renewed by the Holy Spirit]; the old things [the previous moral and spiritual condition] have passed away. Behold, new things have come [because spiritual awakening brings a new life]." The initial preparation, therefore, requires us to relinquish some old things so we can take hold of the new. I am an avid fan of the Hallmark channel and they often illustrate movies depicting some local girl meeting and marrying royalty. I recently watched one of these movies and focused intently on all the preparation that went into this girl becoming a royal bride. It was so intense that the royal parents had chosen from birth to who their son would be betrothed. Though this and most of these movies, usually end with the local girl be- coming a royal bride, at some point it becomes tiring for that bride to indulge in all the preparation. However, regardless of how long it takes, she musters all that is required to fit into the royal family to which she has been betrothed. Sometimes this preparation and eventual marriage even manages to push the family to which she was born into the background, so her new royal family can take center stage in her life.

Sequentially, Esther's experience in Persia falls between Ezra chapters 6 and 7 (revisiting of Jewish refugees from Babylon and Persia to Jerusalem in 538 B.C. under Zerubbabel in Ezra 1-6); and the second revisit led by Ezra in 457 B.C. (Ezra 7-10). Although Esther comes after Nehemiah in the Bible, the actions take place thirty years prior to Nehemiah's return to Jerusalem (444 B.C.) to reconstruct the wall. The importance of Queen Esther is recognized, not only as a result of her saving her people, but also in protecting their security and value in an unfamiliar territory. If Esther and her Jewish people (which included Nehemiah), had perished in Persia, the remainder left in Jerusalem may not have recreated their city.

Therefore, it is safe to say, her actions and reactions saved her nation and people from ultimate doom.

Esther, therefore, had to undergo major preparation to become worthy to be the first pick by the king. Though only a Jewish orphan maiden, she had to step up to the plate and consent to the royal adorning necessary for her to take her place in king Xerxes' king- dom. Before she could even be chosen she had to become a part of the royal harem, placed under the charge of the king's eunuch, who would assure she received the perfect adorning to walk in her regal position. As a result of her magnificent beauty (inner and outer), she immediately won the favor of the king. This, though, was not sufficient to render her Queen. She had to undergo beauty treatments and eat special foods to purify her inside and out. Esther 2:9 declares *"Now the young woman pleased Hegai and found favor with him. So he quickly provided her with beauty preparations and her [portion of] food, and he gave her seven choice maids from the king's palace; then he transferred her and her maids to the best place in the harem."* It was obvious that the treatment would be intense and as a result her former way of life had to be placed on the back burner for a season.

This treatment process was only the preliminary to her actually being seen by the king, or chosen to be his royal bride. *"Now when it was each young woman's turn to go before King Ahasuerus, after the end of her twelve months under the regulations for the women—for the days of their beautification were completed as follows: six months with oil of myrrh and six months with [sweet] spices and perfumes and the beauty preparations for women— then the young woman would go before the king in this way: anything that she wanted was given her to take with her from the harem into the king's palace. In the evening she would go in and the next morning she would return to*

23

the second harem, to the custody of Shaashgaz, the king's eunuch who was in charge of   the concubines. She would not return to the king unless he delighted in her and she was summoned by name" (Esther 2:12-14). There are several things to take note of in this preparation process to gain clarity of just how extreme it was. First and foremost is the fact that it was not a one hour make-over where make-up was applied just to the outer face in about an hour, but the ritual lasted an entire year. Secondly, there was very specific beauty treatments applied during the first six months and another set of oil treatments for the second six months. The third and most important part of the process was that she could not go before the king unless she was summoned by name. These were specific regulations had to be followed to the letter, before Esther could even be considered for the position as Queen.

We too, my sister Queens have been called to the harem that includes women from all walks of life. Our most distinguishing feature is the fact that we have been chosen by the King of all kings to this royal destination. Several scriptures speak to this royal choosing.

But you are A CHOSEN RACE, A royal PRIESTHOOD, A CONSE-CRATED NATION, A [special] PEOPLE FOR God's OWN POSSESSION, so that you may proclaim the excellencies [the wonderful deeds and virtues and perfections] of Him who called you out of darkness into His marvelous light. (1 Peter 2:9 AMP)

Before I formed you in the womb I knew you [and approved of you as My chosen instrument], And before you were born I consecrated you [to Myself as My own]; I have appointed you as a prophet to the nations. (Jeremiah 1:5 AMP)

Blessed and worthy of praise be the God and Father of our Lord Jesus Christ, who has blessed us with every spiritual blessing in the heavenly realms in Christ, 4 just as [in His love] He chose us in Christ [actually selected us for Himself as His own] before the foundation of the world, so that we would be holy [that is, consecrated, set apart for Him, purpose-driven] and blameless in

24

His sight. (Ephesians 1:3-4 AMP)

We have been set apart from ordinary women by our extra ordinary King in order to belong to His royal entourage. This royal calling equips us to walk circumspectly into our elevated destiny as Queens. Before we were born the King determined who we would be and His goal is for us to live in agreement with His majestic will. Our role is to allow His inspired writers of the Word to prepare us to meet Him face to face. This equipping may, at times, cause discomfort and like the chosen woman in the hallmark movie, we may become frustrated. However, like her we too must submit to this royal treatment, recognizing the end result is an encounter with our King.

During Esther's era any one that was to be appointed Queen had to experience a year of planning preceding the ceremony of crowning [Esther 2:3, 6-13]. Esther underwent "a six-month treatment with oil of myrrh and six months with perfumes and other aloes". One Bible version says as "...with olive oil and myrrh..." In early times, the standard woman's fragrance was her anointing oil.

The spiritual implication of this ritual is that Queen Esther immersed in this oil for half of the year before her appearance before the King. This is comparable to our cleansing, dying to self, and preparation for the KING of kings. We must prepare to meet Him, no matter how grueling the preparation may seem at times. Our ex- ample can be seen in Christ Himself, when He came to earth born of a virgin. The "wise men from the east" honored the Christ child with gifts of gold, frankincense, and myrrh [Matthew 2:11]. The gospels tell that prior to His death, Jesus was presented myrrh combined with wine, which he declined, and that subsequent to His death Jesus' body was treated with "an assortment of myrrh and aloes." Frankincense is said to be connected with Christ's function as our intercessor (the bowl of incense in Revelation 5:8 is frankincense, which represents the prayers of the saints), and myrrh connected with His anguish and death. In Song of Solomon 3:6, the writer makes reference to the bridegroom (Jesus) as *"who is He coming in a pillar of smoke smelling of myrrh & frankincense?"* Numerous people have suggested that the gold, frankincense, and myrrh represent the three roles Jesus plays in that order: King, Priest and Prophet.

Therefore, in order to prepare for our Queenly anointing we too must immerse ourselves in the oils required for our meeting with the King of kings. There is a requirement for each one of His daughters to be presented before Him on that great day and in preparation for the glorious event, we are being submerged while we wait. I suppose you could call us "ladies in waiting". For some, while we wait, the oil is more intense than for others, however, we must endure the bitter and the sweet to receive our royal crown.

Sometimes the anointing we receive to carry our cross seems unbearable, but we must keep our minds on the palace like Queen Esther did. The Bible doesn't really specify how long it took Esther to get to the palace, but we do know the Jewish people were in exile for a very long time. Since Esther was raised by her cousin Mordecai, it would appear she had become an orphan, which though not mentioned as such, was part of her anointing. Though it seemed she was being chosen as Queen on the heels of Vashti, God was orchestrating her destiny. There are other women of the Bible who had unusual and sometimes seemingly hurtful anointing as well, however, God allowed major anointing for amazing providence.

Naomi

In the book of Ruth, this great woman exhibited enormous courage in following her husband's decision to move from Bethlehem in a time of famine to the land of Moab, which was more fruitful. However, this move was detrimental, yet pivotal at the same time, in Naomi's life, as she suffered major losses starting with her husband and then her only two sons. At a glance, this looked like a major tragedy and it was to Naomi at the time. It was so painful she became bitter towards her King. Though her name originally meant pleasantness, her life events caused her to change her name to Mara, meaning bitter, when she returned to her homeland. When her daughter-in-law Ruth decided to return home with Naomi, it became the turning point of her anointing to face her King. Though the turmoil seemed unbearable at the time, it was the bitter sweet perfume needed for her anointing to enter into the kingdom as a trailblazer for her Queenly sisters who would follow. (Read the book of Ruth)

Deborah

As the only female judge mentioned in the Bible, she had a very special anointing that was required before entering the palace to meet the King of kings. Her name means Queen Bee and the beholder of beauty, which is an indication of the special perfumes that would be necessary for her preparation. She was not only a judge but a prophetess, which designated her to hear messages from God and communicate His will to the people. She had a great relationship with God, which was the greatest part of her anointing. She was given the task, as leader of Israel and the one who settled disputes, to tell Barak that the Lord commanded him to lead an attack. She knew that God would go before as guide assuring that this endeavor would not fail. As a result of Barak's reluctance to carry out the assignment alone and asking for Deborah's assistance, the Lord would hand Sisera over to a woman. Her anointing perfume and oil of strength gave her the courage to help lead a nation. (Read Judges 4)

Sarah

Sarah was yet another woman of the Bible whose Queenly anointing would render her competent to face the King of kings. She was the only woman in the Bible whose name was changed by God Himself, from Sarai (my princess) to Sarah meaning princess to all. Her anointing with oils and perfumes would eventually render her royalty in becoming the mother of kings of people. Her unique anointing would set her in a position of becoming a part of the lineage of Jesus Christ the Savior. However, this position did not come easy or without a great measure of patience. Sarah was promised a son in her old age, whose name was to be called Isaac and a covenant was to be established by God with him and his descendants. When Sa- rah first received this promise, the Bible said she laughed, because she felt this was the most preposterous thing she had ever heard. However, after much waiting and several detours on her journey to the heavenly palace, the biggest one being to offer her hand maid to her husband; she eventually gave birth to the promised seed. Thus, she was a pioneer for us who would follow, in embracing her Queenly anointing for destiny. (Read Genesis 12-16)

Hannah

The name Hannah means favor or grace, which is the epitome of what it would take for her to embrace her Queenly anointing in going in to meet the King of kings. She was one of the two wives given to Elkanah; however, she was unable to bear him children while his other wife bore many. Hannah is known best for her great faith in praying and believing that God would hear and give her the son she so desired. Therefore, the main feature of her anointing rested in her lifestyle of faith. For years she was ridiculed by Peninnah, Elkanah's other wife, for her infertility, but she exercised restraint and an extra measure of grace in not responding to her tormentor. Her suffering through infertility and eventual unceasing prayer were the anointing perfumes and oils that would make her a forerunner in entering the heavenly palace. Her prayer of faith would not only allow her to conceive and bear a son, but five other children. When Hannah pledged an oath to give her child back to God, this was the catalyst that granted her favor with the King who blessed her with five other children. (Read 1 Samuel 1:1-2:11)

These and other examples have set the stage for what it means to prepare for our royal lineage. It is obvious that the preparation we must each face will be individually different with the end result being a royal encounter with our heavenly King. Some of us will be resolute in preparing, while others will challenge the difficulties that we must encounter to receive the anointing. Regardless of what it takes we must exhibit the mindset of our forerunners, to set our face towards the prize and not look back. Though the oils and perfumes of life that we must encounter will not always be easy or palatable, we must endure so we can enter the heavenly palace and meet the King of all kings.

How are you preparing for your royal lineage?
****

Notes

Walking in the Meaning of Our Name

When we contemplate our destiny it is imperative that we remember the meaning of our names and how we can either align it with our destiny, or invoke changes that will help in the alignment. Esther's name was very instrumental in her vocation as Queen. Her original name Hadassah means compassion and Esther means star, and from the depiction in the book named after her, she lived up to the meaning of her name in the Persian kingdom by being a compassionate star. Esther had a hidden strength built into the core of her being. This strength was as a result of what her name meant. Though a compassionate woman, who was revealed in her allegiance to her people and especially her care giver; she was also a star in carrying out her duties, realizing that in doing so she could lose her very life. Esther, therefore, saw beyond the peripheral pretense that called itself actuality and broke ground for her people by entering the king's domain to converse with him.

Though not really mentioned in the text, research showed her biological father died before she was born and her mother died in child-birth. Thus, she came into the world with the void of having no parents. We are reminded by Heller (2003), that the situation of her birth was no accident. The estrangement and isolation were tools that would be utilized to enable her to become who she was. The root of her Hebrew name *Ester*, is *Saiter* which means concealment. Therefore, her complete name spoke of the very essence of who she was. She was able to penetrate through concealment to find God in the midst of His Spirit. Esther was a master of piercing through what things seemed like in the natural. In her years of aloneness this must have been the weapon she utilized to get to the reality of who God was, even when He seemed to be nowhere to be found. The only real and lasting parent she knew was God. She saw Him in every circumstance of her life. No matter what our name means, we all have places of barrenness, and rather than permit them to lead us to resentment, we need to learn to embrace them as attached to the meaning of our names, leading us to ultimate destiny where we meet the King.

I venture to ask the Queens in the kingdom of God what is the meaning of their names. Sometimes we find that our names have offensive and even insulting meanings. I researched the meanings of some names and found some female names with negative meanings. For example, the name Miriam means bitter and so does Mara and Molly, yet many continue to give these names to their beautiful daughters. If one wanted to reverse the verdict on the dilemma that comes with the name meaning bitter, they would need to embrace a spirit of sweetness and reveal that sweetness through their actions. The list below will give you more names that depict a negative aura such as:

Cecelia = blind
Claudia = lame
Deidra = sorrowful
Emily = rival
Leah = weary

Lola = lady of sorrows

Mallory = unlucky

Portia = pig

Mary = rebellion

Rebecca = "to bind" "to tie" "to snare"

As you scan the names you will probably run across names of loved ones or even your own name, and wonder how you could change the course that this destiny implies. The answer lies in embracing the essence of God like Esther did. Her very birth was indicative of the name solitude and aloneness, yet her actions as Queen allowed her to save a nation. When we think of a name like Mary, which happened to be the mother of our Savior, we recognize how even a teenage girl whose destiny was to bear Him had to turn from rebellion, what her name means, to obedience in taking on this awesome task.

If we were to examine all these names, the women who bear them would all need to reverse the verdict. Cecelia would need to revert to verses that declare sight like *"Open my eyes [to spiritual truth] so that I may behold Wonderful things from Your law"* (Psalm 119:18). Portia whose name means pig would need to be reminded that she is beautiful in the sight of God, declaring to herself daily, *"I will give thanks and praise to You, for I am fearfully and wonderfully made; Wonderful are Your works, And my soul knows it very well* (Psalm 139:14). Claudia who means lame and is a name that we hear often, would need to abort that lameness by dispensing of that meaning and memorizing scriptures like *"I can do all things [which He has called me to do] through Him who strengthens and empowers me [to fulfill His purpose—I am self-sufficient in Christ's sufficiency; I am ready for anything and equal to anything through Him who infuses me with inner strength and confident* peace.]" (Philippians 4:13). Deidra, the one whose name means sorrowful would need to memorize *"For His anger is but for a moment, His favor is for a lifetime. Weeping may endure for a night, But a shout of joy comes in the morning"* (Psalm 30:5). Emily, whose name means rival would need to acquaint herself with *"So, as God's own chosen people, who are holy [set apart, sanctified for His purpose] and well-beloved [by God Himself], put on a heart of compassion, kindness, humility, gentleness, and patience [which has the power to endure whatever injustice or unpleasantness comes, with good temper]; bearing graciously with one another, and willingly forgiving each other if one has a cause for complaint against another; just as the Lord has forgiven you, so should you forgive. Beyond all these things put on and wrap yourselves in [unselfish] love, which is the perfect bond of unity [for everything is bound together in agreement when each one seeks the best for others]* (Colossians 3:12-14).

Though Emily has always been a well-liked name, the meaning denotes rivalry, with competition and contention. Therefore, this woman bearing this name would need to be completely fueled by a scripture like: *"This is my commandment that you love and unselfishly seek the best for one another, just as I have loved you. No one has greater love [nor stronger commitment] than to lay down his own life for his friend. You are my friends if you keep on doing what I command you. I do not call you servants any longer, for the servant does not know what his master is doing; but I have called you [My] friends, because I have revealed to you everything that I have heard from My Father"* (John 15:12-15).

The Biblical character Leah was the wife of Jacob through a deception on the part of her father, Laban. Her name left a legacy of weariness for those who would bear the name after her; therefore, they would need to be familiar with *"Come to me, all who are weary and heavily burdened [by religious rituals that provide no peace], and I will give you rest [refreshing your souls with salvation]. Take my yoke upon you and learn from Me [following Me as My disciple], for I am gentle and humble in heart, and* YOU WILL FIND REST *(renewal, blessed quiet)* FOR YOUR SOULS. *For My yoke is easy [to bear] and my burden is light"* (Matthew 11:28-30). Though Lola has always been one that I liked and I even know a couple people with that name. However, the name indicates a lady of sorrows and the woman bearing this name would be advised to take hold of *"Beloved, do not be surprised at the fiery ordeal which is taking place to test you [that is, to test the quality of your faith], as though something strange or unusual were happening to you.* ¹³ *But insofar as you are sharing Christ's sufferings, keep on rejoicing, so that when His glory [filled with His radiance and splendor] is revealed, you may rejoice with great joy* (1 Peter 4:12 -13).

Another familiar name with a negative meaning would be Mallory, which means unlucky. The Bible does not make reference to luck, but instead speaks continuously about blessings. Therefore, this woman would do well to take hold of the prayer of Jabez, which declares *"Oh that You would indeed bless me and enlarge my border [property], and that your hand would be with me and you would keep me from evil so that it does not hurt me!" And God granted his request* (1 Chronicles 4:10).

In essence, it is possible to reverse the verdict on whatever negative connotation our name has, in an effort to walk boldly and positively into our destiny, or we can embrace those positive names we have been given, in an effort to drive us to where God would have us to be in accomplishing His will for our lives. There is no doubt that God has made each one of us with a specific purpose in mind and it has a lot to do with our names, whether they were strategically or haphazardly thought of by our parents. I am almost positive my parents did not think about the meaning of my name when they called me Sharon. However, when I investigated the meaning of my name and found a form of the name meaning "vision of beauty, grace and love", I was elated to know that haphazardly my parents named me what God destined me to be. I quickly realized that this had nothing to do with my outward appearance, but more so that inner part of me that would eventually exude those characteristics.

Women of God, there are a part of us that at times, just want to run away from our names, because of the load we must bear or the issues conjured up by them. However, when we take a deeper look at the women of the Bible and how they lived up to the meaning of their names, even when they had negative connotations, it gives us hope. I was sent a text message recently that spoke to this instance and though the author was unknown, it fits perfectly with what I am seeking to convey to the Queens reading this very inspirational book. It reads as follows:

Be an *Esther*, bold and courageous enough to stand for the truth, to voice your opinion and fight for the good of others, even when it means to sacrifice yourself. If God has put you in a position, it is for a purpose. Never be afraid to heed that inner voice.

Be a *Ruth*, loyal in all your relationships, walk the extra mile and don't quit when things get tough. Someday, you'll see why it was all worth the effort.

Be a *Lydia*, let your homes be open, let your hands be generous, let your hearts be big enough to help anyone in need. Joy is greatest when shared.

Be a *Hannah*, never cease to pray. It will never be in vain.

Be a *Mary*, humble and submissive. You don't have to be great for God to use you, you just need to obey.

Be a *Dorcas*, use your talents, however small it may seem; to bring a smile on someone's face. You'll never know

how much it can mean to someone.

Be an *Abigail*, remember how each decision can turn your life around for good or bad. Be wise.

Be an *Elizabeth*, never doubt what God can do. Miracles do happen.

Be a *Mary Magdalene*, never let your mistakes and judgments of other people stop you from experiencing true joy.

Be a *Rebekah*, never forget that true beauty lies within. Draw your man closer to God through your character.

Be a *Deborah*, fight and stand up for your right and that of your nation. Ask for the grace to always be on the winning side. You are born to reign and rule.

These great Biblical Queens make it clear that regardless of your name and the difficulties you may have to endure, when you set out to embrace your Queenly anointing you will be blessed. They are the examples that God gives us in His Word to emulate, and when we do He promises victory on every terrain. It is absolutely clear what God is saying to His Queens:

Dare to be an Esther, so you can take hold of boldness and courage, defying all odds.

Dare to be a Ruth, and be loyal in walking that extra mile, reaching for destiny.

Dare to be a Lydia, being generous to open your home, entertaining angels.

Dare to be a Hannah, praying unceasingly, an intercessor to the core.

Dare to be a Mary, filled with humility and obedience, being resolute in your thoughts.

Dare to be a Dorcas, talented yet graceful, being a blessing to many.

Dare to be an Abigail, decisive and wise, exhibiting faith in times of fear.

Dear to be an Elizabeth, with no time for doubting, miracles are on the horizon.

Dare to be a Mary Magdalene, turning mistakes into detours, on your way to real joy.

Dare to be a Rebekah, a vision of inner beauty; God is building your character.

Dare to be a Deborah, a fighter in the kingdom, no war is too big.

When God made us He knew exactly what He was doing and molded us to be Queens. I can clearly hear Him saying today, unmask my Queens, grab hold of your names and dare to be whoever I called you to be.

How does the meaning of your name impact your walk as a Queen?

****

Notes

_____

_____

_____

_____

_____

_____

_____

_____

_____

_____

_____

_____

_____

_____

_____

_____

_____

_____

_____

_____

_____

_____

_____

_____

_____

_____

Submitting to the Royal Calling

B efore Esther could become Queen of Persia she had to submit to the calling. Think about it, she was what seemed like a lowly orphan being raised by her cousin, yet God had a plan for her to be a Queen. Though her cousin saw this as her destiny, it couldn't come to pass until she submitted to the call. The book of Esther in chapter 2 depicts a search being made of all the young virgins in Persia to decide who would be fitting for the Queenly role. We must keep in mind that Esther's original heritage was that of a Jew, which made her part of the deported people banished to Persia. In essence, she was not befitting what one would look for when searching for the Queen of a nation. However, her Daddy was the King of all kings and He had a royal plan. These beautiful maidens, who included Esther, would be placed under the care of the king's eunuch who was in charge of the women. They would go through their period of treatment, as specified earlier, before parading before the king to see who would be chosen. This was the ritual that had to be followed, but God had the ultimate plan for Esther to be Queen. The plan, however, required her submission to the call, because God does not force us to do anything, He gives us choices.

The narrative depicts Esther as being so strikingly beautiful that she immediately won the favor of the one placed in charge of the women. It was obvious to everyone that she was fit to be Queen, but Esther was given the mandate of submitting to this tremendous call and at first it seemed unsure as to whether her answer would be yes. She won so much favor that she was given seven handmaidens and given the best place in the harem. Esther submitted to the call, following her cousin's instructions, in not letting her identity as a Jew be found out. She was not only cared for in the palace, but her cousin watched over her carefully as well. The Bible says *"Everyday he walked back and forth near the courtyard of the harem to find out how Esther was doing and what was happening to her"* (Esther 2:11).

Though she was Queen she recognized she couldn't accomplish the task without her guardian cousin. As the story unfolds it seems Esther was provided anything she wanted, once she submitted to the call to be Queen. However, she was not allowed to return to the king unless he summoned her by name. The remarkable thing about Esther was her meek and humble spirit. She asked for nothing above what she was given and as a result won the favor of many. In order to be chosen she was taken to the king and the scripture declares *"the king was attracted to her more than any of the other women, and she won his favor and approval"* (Esther 2:17). Esther was then crowned Queen of Persia over all other women that paraded before the king. Her submission to the call granted her favor.

We too have been summoned to be royalty as Queens in God's kingdom, but like Esther, we must submit to the call. Since the call is for every woman who accepts Christ as Savior, there is no excuse, regardless of age, social standing, race or culture. Our King does not discriminate and has room for all His maidens.

However, He forces none of us to submit, but give us the choice to do so. Herein is where the problem lies, in the area of our choices. As a young girl of 10 years old, which was more than 47 years ago, I made the verbal choice to become one of His Queens, without choosing from my heart. The dilemma was I had no idea what it meant to be a Queen. As I listened to a radio program back then, I recall hearing the speaker say if I didn't accept Christ as Savior I would be left behind. Therefore, in fear I begged my older sister to lead me to Christ. She did a fantastic job in leading me in the sinner's prayer, but I felt no different after that, I was just comforted in the fact that I wouldn't be left behind and go to hell, even though I didn't understand the concept of hell at the time.

Needless to say, those formative years were spent in confusion as I battled with all the distractions that came my way, especially as a teenager. When people would ask me, I would say I was a Christian, but in my mind I still wondered what that meant. There was something missing, I had not really submitted to the Queenly call. It wasn't until years later that I made the decision to submit and realized that I had won favor with the King long ago, but He had been waiting patiently for me to submit to the call.

When we look at Esther, along with all the Biblical women mentioned earlier, we recognize that no matter who they were there was a specific Queenly calling on their lives that they had to submit to before being able to embrace their royal vocation. We are all given different and unique assignments by the King, some more difficult than others, however, we have to submit before we can walk in our profession.

However, we must first know what our calling is. Sometimes, as a result of confusion or even envy we run after and submit to the wrong profession and as a result lose our way. Jeremiah 29:11 declares *"for I know the plans and thoughts that I have for you,' says the* LORD, *'plans for peace and well-being and not for disaster to give you a future and a hope.* Though a very concise scripture, it gives clarity to the fact that God has a plan for each of His daughters and regardless of what it feels like, the plan is not intended to bring hurt, but to promote hope for all His Queens. Therefore, when faced with adverse situations, we must concede in our pursuit to submit to our royal call. We too, like Esther, must be careful when placed in high positions, not to allow them to make us prideful. God has placed guardians all around us to guide us into our royal destiny, but we can't get puffed up in the middle of greatness, because we will miss the mark, thus causing someone else to be used (Esther didn't change and neither should we).

Every example of daughters of the King given in the Bible has been given a specific call as it pertains to their duty in the kingdom. Esther was called to rescue her people, despite the fact that it could have caused her life. She was so willing to submit that she affirmed in Esther 4:16 *"I will go to the king, though it is against the law; and if I perish, I perish"*.

How many of us who claim to be Queens in God's regime would be willing to perish for the cause of submitting to our calling. Some of us have made major sacrifices so far in our lives and though it felt like a death sentence, we are still alive and well and able to tell about it. As I wrote this portion of the book I came across a poem that I think answers the why of women and all that we go through to honor our roles as Queens called by our Master the King of kings.

I recall speaking to a male friend and trying to answer the question of why women cry so easily. This poem made me realize that crying is a big part of our calling and when we submit our tears to God our King, He makes us stronger. Therefore, I beckon you to cry dear Queens knowing in this you are submitting to your King. The poem goes like this:

Why do Women Cry?

A little boy asked his mother, "Why are you crying?" "Because I'm a woman," she told him.

"I don't understand," he said. His Mom just hugged him and said, "And you never will."

Later the little boy asked his father, "Why does mother seem to cry for no reason?"

"All women cry for no reason," was all his dad could s a y . The little boy grew up and became a man, still wondering why women cry. Finally he put in a call to God. When God got on the phone, he asked, "God, Why do women cry so easily?"

God said, "When I made the woman she had to be special. I made her shoulders strong enough to carry the weight of the world, yet gentle enough to give comfort. I gave her an inner strength to endure childbirth and the rejection that many times comes from her children. I gave her a hardness that allows her to keep going when everyone else gives up, and take care of her family through sickness and fatigue without complaining. I gave her the sensitivity to love her children under any and all circumstances, even when her child has hurt her very badly. I gave her strength to carry her husband through his faults and fashioned her from his rib to protect his heart. I gave her wisdom to know that a good husband never hurts his wife, but sometimes tests her strengths and her resolve to stand beside him unfalteringly. And finally, I gave her a tear to shed. This is hers exclusively to use whenever it is needed." "You see my son," said God, "the beauty of a woman is not in the clothes she wears, the figure that she carries, or the way she combs her hair. The beauty of a woman must be seen in her eyes, because that is the doorway to her heart - the place where love resides."

- Author: Unknown

As I read this poem I realized how important our calling is as Queens and the sacrifices we are required to make in fulfilling our duties, at times to the point of tears. We are called on in life to play so many different roles and sometimes we get tired and frustrated, however, we must stand with courage. We must realize that once we submit to the anointing, this is when the real war for our lives begins.

Esther's divine moment of providence came by accepting her responsibility to go to the king. However, Mordecai was clear when he told her that she could be the one who saved the people, or not. God will use us only if we are ready—or He will find someone else. I fought with God for many years about doing full time ministry and part time job; because I knew it would mean giving up a regular paycheck and possibly losing my house. When I finally made the decision, God showed He was strong in my life and provides for me moment by moment, and it was never in the way I thought He would.

Going into the king's presence was a difficult task for Esther because she realized it meant she could actually die. In order for us to get into the King's kingdom we too are required a measure of suffering. Psalm 34:19-20 says *"Many hardships and perplexing circumstances confront the righteous, but the Lord rescues us from them all. He keeps all our bones; not one of them will be broken"*. Believing and living right will not keep us from going through hellish situations, because the greater the anointing, the greater the suffering.

God has ordained that we must go through many hardships to embrace our Queenly anointing and enter His kingdom. God will deliver us from our hardships when His purpose for the situation has been accomplished. He will either deliver us by supernatural intervention in this life, or by victorious death that takes us to heaven where there is no more suffering.

Ephesians 6:10-18 declares *"be strong in the Lord [draw your strength from Him and be empowered through your union with Him] and in the power of His [boundless] might. Put on the full armor of God [for His precepts are like the splendid armor of a heavily-armed soldier]; so that you may be able to [successfully] stand up against all the schemes and the strategies and the deceits of the devil. For our struggle is not against flesh and blood [contending only with physical opponents], but against the rulers, against the powers, against the world forces of this [present] darkness, against the spiritual forces of wickedness in the heavenly (supernatural) places. Therefore, put on the complete armor of God, so that you will be able to [successfully] resist and stand your ground in the evil day [of danger], and having done everything [that the crisis demands], to stand firm [in your place, fully prepared, immovable, victorious].*

So stand firm and hold your ground, HAVING TIGHTENED THE WIDE BAND OF TRUTH (personal integrity, moral courage) AROUND YOUR WAIST and HAVING PUT ON THE BREASTPLATE OF RIGHTEOUS-NESS (an upright heart), and having strapped on YOUR FEET THE GOSPEL OF PEACE IN PREPARATION [to face the enemy with firm-footed stability and the readiness produced by the good news]. Above all, lift up the [protective] shield of faith with which you can extinguish all the flaming arrows of the evil one. And take THE HELMET OF SALVATION and the sword of the Spirit, which is the Word of God". We are admonished in this scripture to put on our armor and be courageous and determined to fight, in order to embrace our Queenly anointing. This requires being willing to give our lives for the cause of being anointed Queen.

Satan has devised a plan to steal, kill and destroy the plan of God for our lives, and he is not about to abort his plans, so we can't abort the plan of God either. We have to be bold in telling him to back off and stop taking our stuff. Though there is no mention of God or Satan in the book of Esther, she knew if she wanted to submit to her anointing and come out victorious she would be in for the fight of her life. Satan will not make it easy for us to embrace our anointing because his job description defies anything that God says. Matthew 3:27 says *"No man can enter into a strong man's house, and spoil his goods, except he will first bind the strong man; and then he will spoil his house"*.

Jesus has a great concern to defeat Satan and his demons.

Tying up the strong man (Satan) and robbing his house = setting free those imprisoned to Satan.

Power over Satan = driving out demons.

We need to ask God for a supernatural anointing of His Word, prayer and the Holy Spirit's power to tie up Satan and take our stuff back.

When it feels like we are about to perish in the fight, it is a call for warfare prayer, telling the enemy of our souls to back off. When we know who we are fighting against and we jump in to fight, we can accept the charge Paul gave to his protégé Timothy: *"But as for you, be clear headed in every situation [stay calm and cool and steady], endure every hardship [without flinching], do the work of an evangelist, fulfilling [the duties of] your ministry. I am already being poured out as a drink offering, and the time of my departure [from this world] is at hand, and I will soon go free. I have fought the good and worthy and noble fight, I have finished the race, and I have kept the faith [firmly guarding the gospel against error]. In the future there is reserved for me the [victor's] crown of righteousness [for being right with God and doing right], which the Lord, the righteous Judge, will award to me on that [great] day—and not to me only, but also to all those who have loved and longed for and welcomed His appearing"*. (2Timothy 4:5-8)

The devil is a real foe and he won't just let us have our anointing, we must fight for it. God demands total obedience in this fight for our royal position in His palace. Esther's complete obedience saved God's people from genocide and the reality is she didn't know what would happen when she approached the king. She acted in full obedience and in doing so she saved a nation and received the best reward. Therefore, we don't get a pass on this one; we too must exhibit total obedience in the tasks God has given us to accomplish on this side of heaven. Whatever the hindrances are we must hold un- flinchingly to whatever God gives us to do, totally obeying, come what may.

What has God called you to do?

How are you submitting to the call?

What are some things that hinder you from total obedience?

Who is or are the Mordecai's in your life?

How are you soliciting their guidance, or have you gotten too big in your position to heed their counsel?

Our Queenly call requires answers to these questions so we can fully submit and not waste any more time on our way to meeting the King of kings.

How have you submitted to the royal calling on your life?

****

Notes

Becoming the King's Selection

Becoming the king's selection was no easy accomplishment for Esther. She literally had to give up the lifestyle she knew and was accustomed to, and even change her name. We have to keep remembering as we venture through the story of this particular Queen, that she was a mere orphan girl being raised by her cousin. History records that she was born as a Jewish exile named Hadassah. God knew all along that Haman would plot to destroy the Jews and He used Mordecai to set Esther in place as a way to destroy the plot. The book of Esther is a parable and the characters are symbols as follows:

King Xerxes represents our will (Our King of kings desires us to pursue His will).

Haman represents our flesh (the enemy of our soul).

Queen Esther represents our new nature (*spirit*) in Messiah Jesus (walking in our Queenly anointing as a result of salvation).

Mordecai (who was a foster-father to Esther) represents the Holy Spirit—the Father of our new nature (Our counselor); though we can't see our King right now we can embrace our anointing through the power of the Holy Spirit.

This character study gives us a view of why it is sometimes so difficult for us to walk in our anointing as Queens. It requires that we recognize all the forces against us and take a stand to move in the direction of our royal anointing no matter what it takes.

As we take a closer look at these character roles portrayed in each of our lives, the hope is to get through each hurdle and get to the finish line in our royal lineage, unscathed from the twists and turns of life. The hope is to maneuver through our will and our flesh to get to the place of salvation that yields for us the counsel of the Holy Spirit, who is our ultimate link to our Father, the King.

King Xerxes (our will):

This is symbolic of our lives in the world prior to salvation. According to Psalm 51:5 *"Behold, I was brought forth in [a state of] iniquity; my mother was sinful who conceived me [and I too am sinful]"*. Therefore, regardless of how innocent we may seem when we enter this world we are all born in a state of sin and iniquity that we must fight against, almost immediately. As I watched a very graphic video of my third grandchild's birth, I was almost amazed at the fact that as soon as his head came forth from the birthing canal he was crying.

The sound of crying is what those in the birthing room wait for to exclaim that the child is well. Almost immediately after that miraculous birth, in order to soothe the crying the baby was placed in my daughter's arms desiring to be fed. As newborns we instantly scrounge for pleasure, which comes from being fed. We go through life continuously needing different types of feeding and never really being satisfied by what the world has to offer. Our will takes precedence over almost everything as we rummage around for things to bring us pleasure. It is still amazing to me how we filter our decisions based on our will, and cry out to God when we find ourselves in pain. God's desire for every human is to have peace with Him, but we must fight and overcome our will to get to that place of ultimate peace. The Bible declares in Galatians 5:19-23 *"the practices of the sinful nature are clearly evident: they are sexual immorality, impurity, sensuality (total irresponsibility, lack of self-control), idolatry, sorcery, hostility, strife, jealousy, fits of anger, disputes, dissensions, factions [that promote heresies], envy, drunkenness, riotous behavior, and other things like these. I warn you beforehand, just as I did previously, that those who practice such things will not inherit the kingdom of God. But the fruit of the Spirit [the result of His presence within us] is love [unselfish concern for others], joy, [inner] peace, patience [not the ability to wait, but how we act while waiting], kindness, goodness, faithfulness, gentleness, self-control. Against such things there is no law".* This clearly specifies that there is a war going on between our will (sinful nature), and God's will (fruit of the Spirit). Our end result as royalty in the kingdom is dependent on how desperate we are to kill our will, in an effort to get to what God's will is, in an attempt to ac- quire control of our Queenly anointing.

Haman (our flesh)

Though our will and our flesh are sometimes spoken of synonymously, in this instance I chose to differentiate the two by explaining the will being what we are born with, as explained previously and the flesh as those annoying sinews that attach to us as we make our way through life. The flesh is bothersome because it travels with us from pre-salvation into salvation acting as an umbilical cord that is sometimes so difficult to sever. The apostle Paul made reference to how annoying it was in his own life, therefore, we are not exempt from the stronghold that it sometimes has in our own lives. In Ro- mans 7:14-24, Paul refers to it as a hindrance to him understanding his own actions. He explains that it causes him to perform actions that he literally hates. He explains that nothing good comes from the flesh, because it is a direct descendant of Satan, causing us to do wrong when we desire to do right. It wages war against our minds causing us to be captive to sin, thus trying to destroy our royal ancestry in the family of our Father the King. According to Romans 8:5-8 *"For those who are living according to the flesh set their minds on the things of the flesh [which gratify the body], but those who are living according to the Spirit, [set their minds on] the things of the Spirit [His will and purpose]. Now the mind of the flesh is death [both now and forever—because it pursues sin]; but the mind of the Spirit is life and peace [the spiritual well-being that comes from walking with God—both now and forever]; the mind of the flesh [with its sinful pursuits] is actively hostile to God. It does not submit itself to God's law, since it cannot, and those who are in the flesh [living a life that caters to sinful appetites and impulses] cannot please God".* At times other people, or certain circumstances appear to be frustrating to us; we blame them for all our downfalls. We must come to the point where we stop and say *Wait a minute! Is this my own flesh doing this?* If we really examine that question [through God's light], then we realize what an enemy our flesh is. However, most of us choose not to go through the mental and emotional frustration of admitting to that— because it would mean having to stop to answer these annoying questions.

Is it really circumstances?

Is it really other people? Or,

Is it my own flesh?

The answer to these questions distinguishes real Queens in the kingdom from those who are just counterfeit Queens.

Queen Esther (new nature based on salvation)

Ephesians 6:17 says *"take THE HELMET OF SALVATION, and the sword of the Spirit, which is the Word of God".* When we ask Jesus into our hearts we immediately take on a protective covering for our minds. I sometimes wonder why the apostle Paul uses the analogy of a helmet when referring to salvation. I believe he realized from viewing the Roman soldier's armor that the helmet was a crucial piece of equipment used as protective gear for the soldier's head. Our minds are open battle grounds for the enemy, in that, when he wants to attack, that becomes his main target. Thus, when we embrace our new nature we must ensure that our minds are shielded from the onslaught of the enemy of our souls. Our prayer of salvation should be:

> **Loving Heavenly Father,**
> **We desire your reward of salvation!**
> **Come into our hearts and be the Master of everything!**
> **Change all things and make us new!**
> **We were dead in sin and we desire to be raised to life!**
> **Renew a right and new spirit within us!**
> **Allow our hearts to overflow with the joy of your salvation!**
> **In Jesus' name we pray,**
> **Amen!!!**

If you have not said this, or a prayer similar to this before, you are losing out on your anointing as a Queen in the kingdom. Once this becomes the prayer of our hearts we can walk like an Esther into the presence of our King, knowing we are always welcome into His embrace. As a result of this prayer we are given a new nature and we can boldly approach our King knowing His scepter will always be stretched to greet us.

Mordecai (Holy Spirit)

Once we renounce our will and our flesh and set our face like flint towards Jesus as our Savior, the Holy Spirit takes His rightful place as Counselor in our lives. Most people ask how we can believe in a God we cannot see. The answer lies in the Holy Spirit's role as the third person of the trinity left to guard, guide and protect us. Scripture declares *"And I will ask the Father, and He will give you another Helper (Comforter, Advocate, Intercessor—Counselor, Strengthener, Standby), to be with you forever— the Spirit of Truth, whom the world cannot receive [and take to its heart] because it does not see Him or know Him, but you know Him because He (the Holy Spirit) remains with you continually and will be in you"* (John 14:16-17).

Though the book of Esther was written long before the fulfillment of this scripture, we see the Holy Spirit embellished on every line and page of the book of the Bible. Mordecai was a counselor placed in Esther's life as a result of her orphanage. When Jesus left, He promised we wouldn't be like orphans: *"I will not leave you as orphans [comfortless, bereaved, and helpless]; I will come [back] to you"* (John 14:18). When Jesus made this declaration He knew the presence of the Holy Spirit would be with His daughters, making us aware of His nearness as our King. The fact that Christ makes Himself real to us through the power of the Holy Spirit, should make us worship, love and adore Him as the Queenly daughters that we are.

The circumstances surrounding Esther and her commitment to the anointing was based on the possibility of the king not desiring to see her and thus, having her killed. Our submission to the Queenly anointing is based in the guidance of the Holy Spirit as our ultimate counsel. We should know in our hearts that He will never turn us away, and thus, submit to boldly enter His throne room at any time without being beckoned to do so. Even when all we can muster is a groan as a result of our circumstances we are comforted in knowing *"In the same way the Spirit [comes to us and] helps us in our weakness. We do not know what prayer to offer or how to offer it as we should, but the Spirit*

Himself [knows our need and at the right time] intercedes on our behalf with sighs and groaning too deep for words. And He who searches the hearts knows what the mind of the Spirit is, because the Spirit intercedes [before God] on behalf of God's people in accordance with God's will" Romans 8:26-27). Esther's intercessor between her and the king was Mordecai and the intercessor between us and the King of kings is the Holy Spirit.

Therefore, throughout all the conditions of life, that are sometimes so horrific we can hardly speak, we must be resolute in our minds to let go of our flesh and our will, so we can be equipped with our salvation helmet, through the assistance of the Holy Spirit. This is the formula for us to become the Queenly brides that God created, boldly walking daily into our anointing. It is not surprising to me that God equates His Church to that of being a bride and makes reference in every instance to the church as being "her".

In Ephesians 5:27 He says He wants to *"present her to Himself in splendor, without spot or wrinkle or any such thing, that she might be holy and without blemish"*. Thus, as a result of our Father being the King of all kings, there is a level of preparation required for us to get ready for the royal lineage we are afforded through salvation. Esther was an orphan Jewish maiden, but God had a plan to make her Queen of a nation. This required a making process, which I believe though it resulted in victory, was a painful process at times to endure. How are you being made in the crucible of events God is utilizing to present you as a priceless Queen to those watching your journey? Have you suffered major losses? Has illness tried to strip you of your pleasure? Do you feel alone and afraid? Do the negative circumstances seem to outweigh the positive ones? Does your weeping seem to be enduring for more than a night? Do you feel that God has forgotten you? Do the stumbling blocks of life seem overbearing? Do your past wrongs seem like they are dictating your future?

Does the price of becoming a priceless Queen seem too high to pay? If any or even all these questions have permeated your journey, I encourage you today **"not to quit"**.

No matter how difficult it may seem, you are in the process of becoming the King's selection as Queen. When the fire gets hot in the making process, that's when we are learning the most about whom we are and our purpose as Queens in the kingdom of God.

How are you performing?

****

Notes

_____

_____

_____

_____

_____

_____

_____

_____

_____

_____

_____

_____

_____

_____

_____

_____

_____

_____

_____

_____

_____

_____

_____

_____

_____

Embracing Our Queenly Anointing

Someone Knows My Anointing

Though Esther had to go through the loss of her parents and suffer being in exile with her people, there was an anointing on her life that had to be fleshed out. Thus, the conditions of her life were orchestrated by God, because He is the One who knew her anointing. As we take another glimpse of Esther's life, she enters the story when the king called for a national beauty pageant to be held in an effort to find a replacement for the beautiful Queen Vashti. After being in exile with her people, Esther was taken with other young women to a citadel (castle), where they were to be prepared to meet the king so he could make his choice of a new Queen. Esther's striking beauty won her favor with Hegai the one placed in charge of the women. As a result she was granted special favor. She, how- ever, was very careful not to let anyone know about her Jewish background, as she was instructed to do by her cousin Mordecai, because he knew she would face great danger if anyone knew she was a Jew. When it was the appointed time Esther was brought before the king and he immediately got lost in her beauty and she was crowned the next Queen. This all happened as a result of God knowing her anointing.

God knows our anointing as well because He created us for it. However, when things get rough as they most times do for daughters of the King, we succumb to the issues instead of recognizing it is all a part of the Queenly anointing we have been given. The tragedy lies in the fact that we forget to take care of the anointing in all seasons of life. Our anointing is not just given for seasons of abundance, but also when we must endure seasons of drought. God pro- vides us with all the equipment necessary to take care of our anointing; we just need to utilize these tools to maintain our Queenly status.

Comprehend the anointing

The Spirit of the Lord GOD is upon me, Because the LORD has anointed and commissioned me To bring good news to the humble and afflicted; He has sent me to bind up [the wounds of] the brokenhearted, To proclaim release [from confinement and condemnation] to the [physical and spiritual] captives And freedom to prisoners, To proclaim [a] the favorable year of the LORD, And the day of vengeance and retribution of our God, To comfort all who mourn, To grant to those who mourn in Zion the following: To give them a [c] turban instead of dust [on their heads, a sign of mourning], The oil of joy instead of mourning, The garment [expressive] of praise instead of a disheartened spirit. So they will be called the trees of righteousness [strong and magnificent, distinguished for integrity, justice, and right standing with God], the planting of the LORD, that He may be glorified. (Isaiah 61:1-3)

In order to wear the Queenly crowns and robes given to us by the King we must understand the anointing bestowed on us for royalty. This scripture is specifically referring to the Messiah and His anointing for ministry on earth, which required being anointed with the Holy Spirit. He was anointed to preach, heal, bring sight to the physically and spiritually blind and set free those who were bound by strongholds. He was the perfect example of who we are sup- posed to be in our royal positions as Queens. We must comprehend this fourfold ministry anointing so we can reach our full potential as Queens.

Fan the anointing into flames

Fan into flame the gracious gift of God, [that inner fire—the special endowment] which is in you through the laying on of my hands [with those of the elders at your ordination]" (2Timothy 1:6).

The gift (charisma) or Queenly anointing given to us by God is like a fire, and like any fire it must be fanned into flame to keep it burning. We are endowed with power from the King through the Holy Spirit to fulfill whatever assignment is entrusted to us a Queens. Hence, the gifts must be fueled by God's grace through devotion and submission to His will for our lives

Guard the anointing

Guard [with greatest care] and keep unchanged, the treasure [that precious truth] which has been entrusted to you [that is, the good news about salvation through personal faith in Christ Jesus], through [the help of] the Holy Spirit who dwells in you (2Timothy 1:14).

Though the anointing has been bestowed on us, we must safe-guard and protect the anointing committed to us, even when there is a great falling away by others and we remain a remnant of those who continue to believe and trust in the King. We, as Queens, must determine to defend our anointing at any cost. Esther guarded her anointing at the detriment of her own life and was willing to do any-thing to assure that God was glorified in her choices. Our Queenly anointing can only be maintained as we continuously attach to the Holy Spirit, who is our helper and counselor, just like Esther attached to Mordecai who was her helper and counselor.

Maintain the anointing

Therefore as you have received Christ Jesus the Lord, walk in [union with] Him [reflecting His character in the things you do and say—living lives that lead others away from sin], having been deeply rooted [in Him] and now being continually built up in Him and [becoming increasingly more] established in your faith, just as you were taught, and overflowing in it with gratitude. (Colossians 2:6-7)

We have established that God has anointed us as Queens in His kingdom for such a time as this; however, although He knows our anointing we must fight in this world to maintain it. Sometimes the obstacles are so overbearing it seems like giving up would be easier than staying in the fight. When we accept Christ we immediately become heirs to the kingdom, but the Hamans (fleshly desires) that we face seek to hinder us from our pursuit of royalty. Staying rooted and grounded in the palace is no easy feat and it requires walking in union with the King. We must set our face like directly towards the palace (heaven) by embracing and clinging to our faith. There is a reward waiting for us in the palace, but in order to receive it we must take the stance that if we perish we perish.

Reality of the anointing

As for you, the anointing [the special gift, the preparation] which you received from Him remains [permanently] in you, and you have no need for anyone to teach you. But just as His anointing teaches you [giving you insight through the presence of the Holy Spirit] about all things, and is true and is not a lie, and just as His anointing has taught you, you must remain in Him [being rooted in Him, knit to Him]. (1 John 2:27)

We are all given a specific anointing to do a special thing for the King and it requires the intervention of our Mordecai (Holy

Spirit). This anointing comes through mandatory instructions given to us in the BIBLE (Basic Instructions Before Leaving Earth). This is our preparation for our royal position in the Palace. We don't really need anyone to teach us extra-biblical doctrine, because we are given the anointing of the Holy Spirit to defend against doctrinal error. We, as daughters of the King must learn from the King's truth and each other through communal teaching and encouraging. The reality of our anointing as Queens comes from our Father the King through His Son Jesus and the counsel of His Spirit.

The oil of the anointing

You shall put the turban on his head and put the holy crown on the turban. 7 Then you shall take the anointing oil and pour it on his head and anoint him." (Exodus 29:6-7); *Now it is God who establishes and confirms us [in joint fellowship] with you in Christ, and who has anointed us [empowering us with the gifts of the Spirit]; 22 it is He who has also put His seal on us [that is, He has appropriated us and certified us as His] and has given us the [Holy] Spirit in our hearts as a pledge [like a security deposit to guarantee the fulfillment of His promise of eternal life].* (2 Corinthians 1:21-22)

Before Esther could enter the king's chambers, she had to be made ready and part of that required being anointed with special oils. Those oils included myrrh oil which can be used as incense, and is also a component of certain perfumes and ointments. The oil was used as an attractor that would draw Esther closer to the king. Our anointing oil helps to prepare us to go into the presence of our King of kings. According to gotQuestions.org (n. d.), "the New Testament Greek words for anoint are chrio, which means to smear or rub with oil and, by implication, to consecrate for office or religious service; and aleipho which means to anoint". Thus, the oil of our anointing is a significant part of who we are as Queens. We have each been given a role to play, and like Esther we have been handpicked by our heavenly King to fulfill our calling. We have been chosen for an exact purpose which requires special preparation with the anointing oil of God. We must, by our example, exude a sweet smelling savor of the One we belong to. Those who are not acquainted with Him should be drawn to Him by the fragrance we radiate as a result of the oil of the anointing.

The provision of the anointing

You prepare a table before me in the presence of my enemies. You have anointed and refreshed my head with oil; my cup overflows. (Psalm 23:5)

The anointing bestowed on us by the King will come in the form of abundance, that we sometimes have trouble containing, because we are so overwhelmed. We pray elaborate prayers, asking God to enlarge our territory and when He does we become inundated with all that He provides. However, His intention is for us to rejoice in the provision of the anointing, realizing when He provides in this way for His daughters He also engulfs us with His presence, so we can take pleasure in the end result of His blessings. The psalmist reminds us that even in the midst of this abundant anointing, we must never cease to remember that there is an enemy prowling and waiting to devour every part of our provision. In the book of Esther the enemy came in the form of Haman and Esther had to recognize his tactics in order to relish her Queenly provisions in the palace. In essence, though the enemy of our souls perceives, resents, and is bothered by our anointing, he is not afforded the opportunity to hinder it.

The joy of the anointing

You have loved righteousness (virtue, morality, justice) and hated wickedness; Therefore God, your God, has anointed you Above Your companions with the oil of jubilation. (Psalm 45:7)

There is a certain joy that comes with the anointing of God upon His Queens. However, the requirement is that we love righteousness and holiness and hate evil. When Esther came to the palace she entered with a pure heart. The king immediately noticed her above all others and quickly identified her as his Queen. It amazes me that so many others stood before him who seemed worthy of the title, but she stood out among the rest. In our quest for the anointing it is imperative that we stand above the rest in whatever the anointing is that we are called to. We must exude joy regardless of what it takes to get us to the palace. Esther had to become an orphan, be raised by Mordecai, be in exile and still remain joyful, in order to be taken into the palace by the king. Some of us have had to endure horrifying circumstances to receive our anointing as Queens. These situations, though crippling in our dark night seasons, must exude joy in us during our morning seasons, so the King can see His reflection in us when He bids us welcome to the palace.

Thus, we learn here that the King already knows our anointing and utilizes different strategies to get us to embrace it for ourselves.

When I Say I am Anointed

When I say I am anointed,
Don't get me wrong;
It's not that I am bragging,
I just know who makes me strong.

When I say I am anointed,
Don't think of it as pride;

It's not that I am prideful,
It's in my King that I choose to abide.

When I say I am anointed,
Don't think I'm trying to impress;
It's not that I have no scars,
They're just covered in the King's caress.

When I say I am anointed,
Don't think of me as rude;
It's not that the wounds don't cut deep,
But the anointing has made me shrewd.

When I say I am anointed,
Don't think it's because there has been no pain;
It's not that I have not endured hurt,
But my King has loosed the chain.

When I say I am anointed,
Don't think it's because I've not been betrayed;
It's not that I've not suffered long,
I just believe I'm fearfully and wonderfully made.

Dr. Sharon Smith

Though at times the things we go through to birth our anointing seem unbearable, we must endeavor to fight in the crucible of pain to enter the birthing room of the palace. The King of kings knows our anointing and He knew it before we were made. Our job is to seize every opportunity to walk with dignity into some of the fiery furnaces we must encounter, knowing we will come forth unscathed in the kingdom.

What is your anointing and how are you fulfilling it?

****

Notes

A Treacherous Plot for my Life

There is an assassination plot out for all God's Queens. *"Do not imagine that you in the king's palace can escape any more than all the Jews. 14 for if you remain silent at this time, liberation and rescue will arise for the Jews from another place, and you and your father's house will perish [since you did not help when you had the chance]. And who knows whether you have attained royalty for such a time as this [and for this very purpose]?"* (Esther 4:12-14) Just because Esther was in the palace and a very important part of the kingdom, she couldn't escape the plot for her life. There was a very strong and influential enemy in the name of Haman who wanted to destroy her people and her. Like any normal person, Esther was afraid and thought about how to get out of going before the king. However, Mordecai, her constant companion and counselor, re- minded her that she was sent to the palace for such a time as this, and if she reneged on the opportunity to embrace her royal position God would find someone else to fulfill the role. I can only imagine how Esther must have felt, realizing that her journey to the palace could end in treachery. Though she was a chosen Queen this could be the ending of her infamous moment and could also lead to her physical death.

Although God is never mentioned in the book of Esther, it is obvious at this climactic moment in the narrative that He was the unmentioned, yet very visible producer, of a book that reads like the plot of a dramatic movie. Regardless of how we want to view this epic book, it is in reality how God views the life of His daughters in the kingdom. Some of us have endured some amazing things to finally grasp our anointing as Queens. Yet God is the unseen producer of every act and scene portrayed in the dramatic movies of our lives. Like Esther, there is a treacherous plot for our lives, and as a result we sometimes shrink back because we are afraid to die. We must realize that to get to the palace we must, face some form of death. Though the enemy of our souls, like Haman, wants to *steal, kill and destroy,* (John 10:10), he can only do as much as God allows. In Job 1:12 God gives Satan instructions concerning Job saying:

"Behold, all that Job has is in your power, only do not put your hand on the man himself." Therefore, though Satan could destroy Job's property, goods and even family, he was not privy to lay a finger on Job. It is the same with us, in that, though the enemy can manage to destroy many tangible things in our lives, he can only touch us as God allows. The treacherous plot that Satan has to consume us can only be accomplished if God allows. However, there are some treacherous things that have attached themselves to us, because we have allowed them. Therefore, there are some things that need to be killed in our lives so they don't kill our anointing.

Kill self

Then Jesus said to His disciples, "If anyone wishes to follow Me [as My disciple], he must deny himself [set aside selfish interests], and take up his cross [expressing a willingness to endure whatever may come] and follow Me [believing in Me, conforming to My example in living and, if need be, suffering or perhaps dying because of faith in Me]." Matthew 16:24

A lot is required in killing self. However, if we don't it's almost definite that the treacherous plot for our lives will be carried out and will succeed. If our desire is to truly walk in our anointing as Queens we must constantly remind ourselves that we have a cross to carry that is a part of the anointing. We must be willing to endure whatever it takes to get to the palace. The mandate is for us to do what Jesus would do, in an effort to embrace royalty. Therefore, we must be willing to possibly suffer, even to the point of death. In essence, when we kill self we are able to become Queens and like Esther, we can say "if I perish I perish".

Kill jealousy

You are jealous and covet [what others have] and your lust goes unfulfilled; so you [b]murder. You are envious and cannot obtain [the object of your envy]; so you fight and battle. You do not have because you do not ask [it of God]. 3 You ask [God for something] and do not receive it, because you ask [c]with wrong motives [out of selfishness or with an unrighteous agenda], so that [when you get what you want] you may spend it on your [hedonistic] desires. (James 4:2-3).

These verses are so attuned to who we sometimes are as women. Our jealous and covetous attitudes sometimes cause us to destroy friendships and even family relationships. We, at times, sit in the church pews defeating our anointing because we desire what others have, instead of recognizing our own anointing. As a result of envy, we sulk and lose interest in our own blessings, causing us to lose our way in the kingdom. When we finally do ask God for something, we ask with ungodly motives, causing God so much displeasure, He has to re-route the royal anointing He so desperately wants to give us.

Kill confusion

For the good that I want to do, I do not do, but I practice the very evil that I do not want. (Romans 7:19)

This verse speaks to our human condition and how we some-times allow confusion to step in and cause us to do wrong when we desire to do right. This confused nature sometimes drives us to a place of despair, hindering our anointing as the Queens God de-sires. We are; therefore, engaged in a spiritual combat between good and evil on the inner part of us, while we engage in a fight against the enemy of our souls—Satan. By utilizing the whispers of the Holy Spirit, the Lord continuously persuades us to do the right thing and relinquish what is wrong.

Kill earthly treasures

Do not store up for yourselves [material] treasures on earth, where moth and rust destroy, and where thieves break in and steal. 20 But store up for yourselves treasures in heaven, where neither moth nor rust destroys, and where thieves do not break in and steal. (Matthew 6:19-20)

Sometimes God allows us to glimpse amazing earthly blessings as a revelation to us that He is treating us like the royalty He created us to be. However, we get so bogged down with the earthly treasures, we forget the Giver, allowing our minds to be consumed. These earthly treasures become our gods, as we tend to forget they are only temporary. This does not mean we shouldn't take care of what God gives us on this side of heaven, but we should not be-come consumed by them. By killing them, we are able to start focusing on our heavenly rewards that will be eternal. I have been privy to seeing some beautiful homes with all the amenities that life has to offer, but the owners still tell me this is not their dream home, endeavoring to get more and more. This mindset keeps us from acquiring the gems God has for us as Queens in His kingdom, be- cause our minds are settled on the temporary instead of the eternal.

Kill relationships

You shall not make for yourself an idol [as an object to worship], or any likeness (form, manifestation) of what is in heaven above or on the earth beneath or in the water under the earth. 9 You shall not worship them or serve them; for I, the LORD your God, am a jealous (impassioned) God [demanding what is rightfully and uniquely mine], visiting (avenging) the iniquity (sin, guilt) of the fathers on the children [that is, calling the children to account for the sins of their fathers], to the third and the fourth generations of those who hate Me. (Deuteronomy 5:8-9)

Friends, parents, siblings, spouses, girl/boy-friends, children, co -workers, bosses, etc. can all become major distractions on our way to our Queenly anointing. The scripture clearly admonishes us to not worship anything or anybody above our King. Yet we find our- selves putting so many people and things in front of Him that we sometimes lose our way to the anointing He has for us. Esther al- most lost her footing when she focused on the earthly king instead of her heavenly King. It is only when she was ready to forfeit the earthly, that she and her people were blessed in the heavenly. We too, as Queens, must be ready to sacrifice some earthly relationships in an effort to embrace Queenly royalty.

Kill desiring the blessings more than the Blesser

But first and most importantly seek (aim at, strive after) His kingdom and His righteousness [His way of doing and being right—the attitude and character of God], and all these things will be given to you also. (Matthew 6:33)

It can be so simple to pray for a precise object repeatedly, but fail to remember about time needed with God. This would be like a husband wanting that special "sexual benefit" he gets from his wife, devoid of giving any occasion to the supplementary ingredients of their relationship. However, we are specifically taught to seek the

Blesser first, knowing that everything else that we need will be given to us. Our royal Queenly anointing is awaiting us, but God requires first dibs because He is a jealous God. When we seek temporary blessings before seeking Him we risk forfeiting eternal blessings and in turn the anointing He has for us.

Kill religiosity

If anyone thinks himself to be religious [scrupulously observant of the rituals of his faith], and does not control his tongue but deludes his own heart, this person's religion is worthless (futile, barren). 27 Pure and unblemished religion [as it is expressed in outward acts] in the sight of our God and Father is this: to visit and look after the fatherless and the widows in their distress, and to keep oneself uncontaminated by the [secular] world. (James 1:26-27)

Religion can be a BIG intrusion on our way to being anointed as Queens. Church/religion can effortlessly become an obstruction to our Queenly heritage. Why? The most important cause is that it is so easy to become consumed with the attraction of church and the activities; viewpoints on the subject of God; but overlook pursuing the King Himself. It is so easy to just attend church just for the sake of it, when we should be attending church to be replenished for our week, worshiping and meditating on God. We become so enticed with the idea of church that we forget the why of church. Thus we end up being religious instead of true daughters of the King seeking to follow and obey Him.

Kill anxiety and worry

Do not be anxious or worried about anything, but in everything [every circumstance and situation] by prayer and petition with thanksgiving, continue to make your [specific] requests known to God. 7 And the peace of God [that peace which reassures the heart, that peace] which transcends all understanding, [that peace which] stands guard over your hearts and your minds in Christ Jesus [is yours]. (Philippians 4:6-7)

The daughter of the King striving for her royal position can easily become overwhelmed with anxiety and worry that result from the issues of life. For Esther it was her concern about being put to death if she entered the earthly king's domain without an invitation. Sometimes, we face adverse situations like sickness, financial devastation, loss of loved ones, loneliness and so much more. The solution here is not to worry or fret, but give it to God. Sometimes, even when we say we let it go, we continue to find ourselves in a state of upset. The Bible tells us that our King's yoke is easy and His burden light and when we become weary we should go to Him. Yet we find that difficult to do and relent to trying to help the Creator of the universe to do His job. In so doing we abandon the peace that He offers as the guard at our hearts' door. We miss out on the blessings offered for our royal lineage.

The Anointing Is On Your Life

God has anointed you from the crown of your head to the soles of your feet.

He has blessed your every waking moment.

You're a true woman of God.

The light that shines so bright from you is radiant with the Holy Spirit.

The anointing that is upon you is placed upon everything and everyone you touch.

There is not a time that anyone could call upon you and you would not come or listen.

For God is an awesome God to have placed an angel such as you here for others.

The words that flow from your mouth are not of you but they are of God.

Anyone can see this, even someone with blind eyes.

You never give up on the fight for the anointing within you to increase.

You pray without ceasing day and night.

You always give God the praise for what he has done in your life and for what he is doing in your life.

Obeying His calling on your life has its rewards you will see.

The enlargement of your territory is just the beginning.

It may seem tough, but being a servant of God is never an easy task.

He did not say it would be.

The tests and trials only come to make you strong.

If you must wear your knees out to muster the strength to do his will.

Do it!!!

For your work is not yet done.

Alone you must go and the strength will come.

You're a true woman of God and the anointing is on your life.

- Suan L. Payne

We have been given a specific mandate concerning our anointing, but there is also a plot out for our lives. It is a treacherous scheme to rid us of any and everything that will make us women of greatness, women of integrity, anointed Queens. Unfortunately, though we try to lay blame on Satan for everything bad in our lives, there are some things we incur on ourselves that must die in an effort to walk as Queens. It is only when we totally surrender to the King in all areas that we embark on a journey of royalty leading us to be Queens. This requires unflinching faith in the King and all that He tells us to do. When Esther decided to throw caution to the wind and trust in God, she was able to overlook the treacherous plot for her life, thus, rendering her the courage to embrace her authentic role as Queen declaring "if I perish I perish".

We all have the ability to courageously live as Queens, but we have to recognize that nothing accomplished wholeheartedly for God is completed without some type of risk. The question is how much risk are we willing to sustain in order to be Queens? This is a question that has to be answered individually, before deciding to enter the ranks of kingdom Queens. As a result, many of us choose the wide easy path as opposed to the narrow difficult path to our anointing. Unfortunately, this keeps us from truly gaining the rewards our King has in store, when we choose to step out in faith and take the Esther risk.

How does knowing there's a treacherous plot for your life affect you as a Queen?

****

Notes

A Treacherous Plot for my Life

Intercession with the King

Esther is referred to, by some commentaries, as a secret agent. Her Hebrew name was Hadassah (the myrtle plant) initially given to her by her Jewish parents. The narrative never gives us a description, or even slightly mentions exactly who her parents were, thus she steps onto the stage as an orphan. She never discloses who she really is in front of king Xerxes until it was absolutely necessary. This Biblical, mysterious woman was humble and unassuming, not quite what we would identify as Queenly qualities. In the story her alias is Esther which means "star" and she absolutely signifies star qualities. Thus, there are magnificent thoughts to be gleaned from this Biblical woman, though she develops from a place of secrecy.

Though she had spent a significant amount of time in the palace when it came time to intercede with the king on behalf of her people she hesitated. She feared for her life, and at this moment probably regretted ever accepting the assignment to vie for Queen of this great nation. She knew that the custom and law for intercession with the king required an invitation, and without it she could possibly be killed. The fear that must have consumed her, most possibly, caused her to reconsider her role as Queen, hoping to possibly even relinquish the crown. She was in, what we would refer to as, a tight spot. She was stuck between a rock and a hard place. It sounds to me like the beautiful Queen was completely and utterly confused. She knew what had to be done, but quaked in her sandals to do it and Mordecai made it even worse by issuing her an ultimatum, which basically said if she didn't step up to the plate, God would assign the task to someone else. He knew, more than Esther, what was required and that she had to complete this task, but he could not force her. She had to make the final decision herself.

There are a few places, especially in the Old Testament where it is said that certain people actually saw God.

Jacob saw God face to face (Genesis 32:30). Moses hid his face because he was afraid to look at God (Exodus 3:6). Again scripture declares, "The Lord spoke to Moses face to face, as a man speaks to his friend" (Exodus 33:11). It also says, "There has not arisen a prophet in Israel like Moses, who the Lord knew face to face" (Deuteronomy 34:10). We read also "in the year king Uzziah died, Isaiah saw the Lord, high and lifted up with his train filling the temple" (Isaiah 6:1). Ok, so is the Bible contradicting itself, because it also says in Colossians 1:15 "He is the image of the invisible God". Paul also wrote, "no one has ever seen God, but God the One and only" (John 1:18). He wrote in his letter to Timothy, "Who alone is immortal and who lives in unapproachable light, whom no one has seen or can see" (1 Timothy 6:16).

After looking at this from a Biblical stance, I realize that sometimes during the Old Testament period God revealed Himself in a Theophany (a physical manifestation to humankind of God), or Christophany (non-physical manifestation of Christ) to a chosen few. This could be clarified as a manifestation of God for the benefit of those He was speaking to. When Esther finally made her decision to intercede with the king, she also decided it was worth it to die over this. None of us can actually see God in the natural, because He is a supernatural, invisible Spirit. However, the Bible says, as a result of His death, burial and resurrection we are given access to His throne room and can intercede for ourselves and others. Hebrews 4:16 says:

"Therefore let us [with privilege] approach the throne of grace [that is, the

throne of God's gracious favor] with confidence and without fear, so that we may receive mercy [for our failures] and find [His amazing] grace to help in time of need [an appropriate blessing, coming just at the right moment]."

Hence, we have gained access to enter the throne room of God and intercede for ourselves and those we are commanded to pray for. Though it is not a face to face interlude like Esther had with the earthly king, it has the potential to bring great things into being. During Levitical times, which were when Esther lived and reigned as Queen, only the high priest was allowed to approach God's presence, and only once a year. The people were not permitted to enter, what was called the Holy of Holies, because of their sins. The sacrificial death of Christ opened the way for bold entry into the King's throne room. As a result of His death and the figurative reference to the curtain being torn in two, we now have access without fear, to intercede with the King.

On account of the beautiful priceless Queens that we are, we're compelled to intercede with the King and we can do so boldly. It is my belief that there are a couple of things that can either make us or break us as the King's daughters:

1) When we are faced with the advent of unrelenting in times of testing
2) Our prayer life.

Though these two crucial occasions are a call to intercession with the King, when we are face to face with them we tend to shrink back and lose heart, giving room to the Haman (antagonist, flesh, Satan etc.) in our lives, who tell us prayer won't change any- thing. Mark 4:15-17 explains the type of heart that receives this seed as:

"Not having any real root in themselves, so they endure only for a little

while; then, when trouble or persecution comes because of the word, immediately they [are offended and displeased at being associated with Me and] stumble and fall away."

Prayer is our lifeline, especially in times of suffering, and the way in which we intercede with our King. The enemy knows this and does everything in his power to deter us from our time of intercession. He interferes with our thoughts, steering us away from prayer and towards worry and doubt. He becomes a constant companion in the war for our thoughts, inflicting thoughts like "why bother to pray? It's senseless." His goal, like Haman's, is to destroy us; he wants us to be cut off from the King and Lover of our souls.

Since we have an everlasting King, unlike the king Esther feared, we are beckoned to embrace our royal lineage as Queens and intercede. In Hebrews 4:14 we are exhorted *"Inasmuch then as we [believers] have a great High Priest who has [already ascended and] passed through the heavens, Jesus the Son of God, let us hold fast our confession [of faith and cling tenaciously to our absolute trust in Him as Savior]."* This is a command to "hold fast our confession of faith". In Hebrews 4:16 we are exhorted *"Therefore let us [with privilege] approach the throne of grace [that is, the throne of God's gracious favor] with confidence and without fear, so that we may receive mercy [for our failures] and find [His amazing] grace to help in time of need [an appropriate blessing, coming just at the right moment]."* This is a command to "approach the throne of grace without fear". Esther needed help for herself and her people; therefore, she had to intercede with the earthly king and did so with the help of her heavenly King. As Queens, in an effort to receive our heavenly anointing, we must intercede with our King on behalf of ourselves and others.

Psalm 110:1 tells us *"The LORD (Father) says to my Lord (the Messiah, His Son), "Sit at My right hand until I make your enemies a footstool for your feet [subjugating them into complete submission]."* It is clear from this scripture that God wants His Queens to sit at His feet in prayer, and that the Hamans' in our lives will become a footstool that we can step on and kill, just like Haman was hung and killed on a gallows, because of Esther's intercession with the king. We cannot ignore the Hamans in our lives, but we cannot give them too much attention either, or allow fear to overtake us. We have been given access to the King's throne room and therefore, must accept our invitation every day to intercede with Him.

Like Esther, God has given us people who we must intercede for and this is part of our anointing as Queens. Hebrews 7:11-19 in explaining the difference between the Old and New Testament priestly ministry said, *"Now if perfection (a perfect fellowship between God and the worshiper) had been attainable by the Levitical priesthood—for under it the people were given the Law—why was it further necessary that there should arise another and different kind of Priest, one after the order of Melchizedek, rather than one appointed after the order and rank of Aaron? 12 For when there is a change in the priesthood, there is of necessity an alteration of the law [concerning the priesthood] as well. 13 For the One of Whom these things are said belonged [not to the priestly line but] to another tribe, no member of which has officiated at the altar. 14 For it is obvious that our Lord sprang from the tribe of Judah and Moses mentioned nothing about priests in connection with that tribe. 15 And this becomes more plainly evident when another Priest arises Who bears the likeness of Melchizedek, 16 Who has been constituted a Priest, not on the basis of a bodily legal requirement [an externally imposed command concerning His physical ancestry], but on the basis of the power of an endless and indestructible Life. 17 For it is witnessed of Him, You are a Priest forever after the order (with the rank) of Melchizedek. 18 So a previous physical regulation and command is cancelled because of its weakness and ineffectiveness and uselessness— 19 for the Law never made anything perfect—but instead a better hope is introduced through which we [now] come close to God.*

The descendants of the tribe of Levi made up the Levitical priesthood in the Old Testament, which was passed from generation to generation. The priesthood of Melchizedek, which is referred to in this scripture, is a new priestly order where Jesus is the High Priest. Through His blood this priesthood is passed on to us as His daughters through our new birth as new women in Christ.

Jesus is the representation for intercessory prayer, who intercedes with God the Father. According to 1Timothy 2:5 which says *"For there is [only] one God, and [only] one Mediator between God and mankind, the Man Christ Jesus."* In essence, Jesus brings us as sinful women in concert with our heavenly King; hence, we can now draw near to the King as a result of the blood of Jesus. We can do so boldly, not cowardly. Therefore, when we intercede with the King we are following the priestly meaning of the Old Testament and the model Jesus set in the New Testament. This requires a certain relationship that can only be accomplished when we spend time with the King. Hebrews 12:14 says *"Continually pursue peace with everyone, and the sanctification without which no one will [ever] see the Lord."* We as daughters of the King and Queens in the kingdom cannot fully embrace our anointing without a certain measure of intimacy with the King. We are now royalty and there is a certain measure of power allotted to us as members of the greatest royal family, where we have legitimate right of entry to the King's throne room. *At once I came under the [Holy] Spirit's power, and behold, a throne stood in heaven, with One seated on the throne!*

And He who sat there appeared like [the crystalline brightness of] jasper and [the fiery] sardius, and encircling the throne there was a halo that looked like [a rainbow of] emerald.

Twenty-four other thrones surrounded the throne, and seated on these thrones were twenty-four elders [a]the members of the heavenly Sanhedrin), arrayed in white clothing, with crowns of gold upon their heads.

Out from the throne came flashes of lightning and rumblings and peals of thunder, and in front of the throne seven blazing torches burned, which are the seven Spirits of God [the sevenfold Holy Spirit];

And in front of the throne there was also what looked like a transparent glassy sea, as if of crystal. And around the throne, in the center at each side of the throne, were four living creatures (beings) who were full of eyes in front and behind [with intelligence as to what is before and at the rear of them].

The first living creature (being) was like a lion, the second living creature like an ox, the third living creature had the face of a man, and the fourth living creature [was] like a flying eagle.

And the four living creatures, individually having six wings, were full of eyes all over and within [underneath their wings]; and day and night they never stop saying, Holy, holy, holy is the Lord God Almighty (Omnipotent), Who was and Who is and Who is to come.

And whenever the living creatures offer glory and honor and thanksgiving to Him Who sits on the throne, Who lives forever and ever (through the eternities of the eternities),

The twenty-four elders (the members of the heavenly Sanhedrin) fall prostrate before Him, Who is sitting on the throne, and they worship Him Who lives forever and ever; and they throw down their crowns before the throne, crying out,

*Worthy are You, our Lord and God, to receive the glory and the honor and dominion, for You created all things; by Your will they were [brought into being] and were created." (*Revelation 4:2-11)

No need for Queens to fear when in intercession, we just have to RUN TO THE THRONE ROOM OF OUR KING!!!

How often do you intercede with the King and how has it impacted your life as a Queen?

****

Notes

Embracing Our Queenly Anointing

Anointed for Such a Time as This

E sther 4:14 declares, *"For if you remain silent at this time, liberation and rescue will arise for the Jews from another place, and you and your father's house will perish [since you did not help when you had the chance]. And who knows whether you have* attained royalty for such a time as this *[and for this very purpose]?"* I don't think Esther really understood why she was in the palace until she was confronted with this major decision to rescue her people from the treacherous plot of Haman. Vashti had been deposed and Esther had taken her place. She had gone through all the ritualistic procedures in an effort to be pleasing to the king, and ultimately be chosen as his next Queen. She was anointed and appointed Queen of Persia, and this was quite an honor in light of her meek beginnings as an orphan and slave girl in exile with her people. Now she has come face to face with the decision that would establish the true reason for her anointing. However, like all of us anointed to be Queens, there are questions that must be answered in an effort to continue our journey and function in our individual roles.

Some questions that require our immediate attention could be: Why are we living where we live? Why are we placed where we are? Why do we attend school where we attend school? Why are we working where we work? Why do we attend the church we attend? If the answers line up correctly, the fact is we do what we do because God has assigned and anointed us for where we are – "for such a time as this."

There are times when we find ourselves in a pivotal moment in our lives, when we have to make strategic decisions concerning our lives that will either make or break us. In basketball it happens when there is a tie in the game with two seconds to go and the player with the ball in hand knows if he misses the basket the game will go into overtime and the other team gets the opportunity to win. In the corporate world it's the event that will either put you over the top or in the red for the economic year. It is that moment in life when we stand still for a moment just to take self-inventory and decide if this is where God wants us to be in order to anoint us for such a time as this. As women in the church universal, I believe we are in a strategic time, where every moment counts. The ball is in our court and how we shoot will be the deciding factor for the game, leading to our Queenly purpose in the kingdom.

So many of us settle for more peasantry roles in the kingdom, thinking they are more easily accomplished, and who needs a Queenly crown with such a high price tag anyway. That attitude has been a great downfall for the church, because there is something remarkable about a Queen accepting her anointing for such a time as this. God created each one of us for a heavenly assignment - a one of a kind purpose that only we can fulfill - like Esther! There is a seemingly impossible mission that only we can accomplish for God - a God appointed function only we can achieve. It requires a definitive answer to each of the questions posed, so we can evaluate our role to establish if we are on the threshold of Queenly greatness.

Why are we living where we live?

"And He made from one man every nation of mankind to live on the face of the earth, having determined their appointed times and the boundaries of their lands and territories."

(Acts 17:26)

Over the years my lifestyle has changed several times. I have

gone from married to single twice, which each time required a change in venue to survive. I have transitioned from being a single mother to just living single, which required being anchored in God to gain my footing. I have put down roots on several occasions, hoping and praying I was in the will of God every time. In essence, I have lived on the edge. I currently live where I live because I am no longer running away from God but to Him. Hence, I am embracing my Queenly anointing for such a time as this. Where we live is a definitive factor as it pertains to how God will use us in His Kingdom. **It is of utmost importance that we, like Esther, be strategically placed where we live so that when God decides to position the ball in our hands, we will be ready to shoot the winning basket—declaring "I have been anointed Queen for such a time as this".**

Why do we attend school where we attend school?

"How much better it is to get wisdom than gold! And to get understanding is to be chosen above silver." **(Proverbs 16:16)**

I sometimes feel like I have been attending school all of my life. However, I started at 3 years old, dropped out of college at 22 years old, and returned at 40 years old with a vengeance, in hopes of attaining all that God would have for me. When I look over the years from 40 until now, I realize it was only then that I really began to seek God about my academic career. The many roles I have played and will play in the future are dependent on being strategically placed in all aspects of life. For me, where I attend must line up with God's plan and as a result I have sought Him on every terrain.

Though I have included school in the questions to be answered, it may not apply to you. However, if it doesn't apply and it was in fact intended by God that you attend, then my suggestion is that you start so your will lines up with the King's will for you as a Queen. **It is of utmost importance that we, like Esther, be strategically placed in the right school (if that's where God wants us), so that when God decides to position the ball in our hands, we will be ready to shoot the winning basket—declaring "I have been anointed Queen for such a time as this".**

Why are we working where we work?

"For I know the plans and thoughts that I have for you,' says the LORD, 'plans for peace and well-being and not for disaster, to give you a future and a hope." (Jeremiah 29:11)

Our profession is of extreme significance to our God and King. As I reflect on all the places where I have worked, especially in the last 18 years, I realize I was intentionally placed in every position by the King. Though I wasn't always sure what was being required, and to me none of the jobs produced major financial gains, God utilized each one to reveal His strength in my own weakness. While working in the public school system I was afforded the opportunity to begin that career working with disabled, autistic children for very little financial rewards. Sometimes there wasn't even enough to pay all the bills, but they miraculously got paid, because I was standing on the promises of God.

As I reluctantly transitioned in 2016 into full-time ministry and part-time work, I could still feel the anointing on my life, though what I was doing seemed humanly ridiculous. As I pen these pages God continues to divulge His secret things that I must know in an effort to be the Queen He requires. I say to you my sister Queens, do not be lackadaisical about where you work, because this too is part of the Queenly journey. Be resolute about working as unto God and not man. You may even have to fight some seemingly impossible battles, but if you persist God will prevail. **It is of utmost importance that we, like Esther, be strategically placed in the workplace so that when God decides to position the ball in our hands, we will be ready to shoot the winning basket—declaring "I have been anointed Queen for such a time as this".**

Why do we attend the church we attend?

"And [His gifts to the church were varied and] He Himself appointed some as apostles [special messengers, representatives], some as prophets [who speak a new message from God to the people], some as evangelists [who spread the good news of salvation], and some as pastors and teachers [to shepherd and guide and instruct], 12 [and He did this] to fully equip and perfect the saints (God's people) for works of ser- vice, to build up the body of Christ [the church]; 13 until we all reach oneness in the faith and in the knowledge of the Son of God, [growing spiritually] to become a mature believer, reaching to the measure of the fullness of Christ [manifesting His spiritual completeness and exercising our spiritual gifts in unity]." (Ephesians 4:11-13)

I believe this might be the most important question of all, as we sometimes tend to attend the churches we do for the wrong reasons. I have had the privilege of attending some great teaching churches, especially in my formative years, when it was crucial to my learning. The Plymouth brethren with its strict teachings helped in forming my spiritual foundation. Though not always the most absolute in their way of operating, the fundamental lessons that I needed growing up were imbedded, forming, what is now, the basis for my hunger and thirst for more of God. My desire for more transitioned me to a Pentecostal church that was second to none in teaching and training its parishioners to go forward in serving. I believe it was in that church where I learned what it meant to truly serve as a Queen in the Kingdom. Wherever I attend in this latter season of my life will always be an outgrowth of all I learned from those former churches, which sprang roots in me so I could bloom wherever I am planted. As Queens, we must be unyielding in our decision as to what church we attend, especially during the influential years of our re-birth in the Kingdom. We cannot be careless about that choice because it sometimes becomes the deciding factor in how we minister as Queens. **It is of utmost importance that we, like Esther, be strategically placed in church so that when God decides to position the ball in our hands, we will be ready to shoot the winning basket—declaring "I have been anointed Queen for such a time as this".**

After Queen Vashti's deposal, the Persian king ordered that a new Queen be chosen. Therefore, a search was started, in the places where all the stunning youthful girls in the empire, who were seemingly entitled to be the new Queen, would be found. Esther had to be in the right place at the right time to be chosen. We too must assure that we are in the right place at the right time so we are not overlooked for the roles we should play as Queens in God's King- dom. As I contemplate what it takes to dig deep and be in the right place to become God's Queen for such a time as this, I realize that the undertaking requires a **Phenomenal Woman**.

Phenomenal Woman by Maya Angelou

Pretty women wonder where my secret lies.
I'm not cute or built to suit a fashion model's size
But when I start to tell them,
They think I'm telling lies.
I say,
It's in the reach of my arms
The span of my hips,
The stride of my step,
The curl of my lips.
I'm a woman, phenomenally.
Phenomenal woman,
That's me.

I walk into a room
Just as cool as you please,
And to a man,
The fellows stand or
Fall down on their knees.
Then they swarm around me,
A hive of honey bees.
I say,
It's the fire in my eyes,
And the flash of my teeth,
The swing in my waist,
And the joy in my feet.
I'm a woman
phenomenally.
Phenomenal woman,
That's me.

Men themselves have wondered
what they see in me.
They try so much
but they can't touch
my inner mystery.
When I try to show them
they say they still can't see.
I say,

It's in the arch of my back,
The sun of my smile,
The ride of my breasts,
The grace of my style.
I'm a woman, phenomenally.
Phenomenal woman,
That's me.

Now you understand,
Just why my head's not bowed.
I don't shout or jump about
or have to talk real loud.
When you see me passing
It ought to make you proud.
I say,
It's in the click of my heels,
The bend of my hair,
the palm of my hand,
The need of my care,
'Cause I'm a woman
Phenomenally.
Phenomenal woman,
That's me.

How are you functioning in your anointing for such a time as this?

****

Notes

Prayer and Fasting Required

The Bible declares that Jesus fasted for forty days in preparation for His earthly ministry and His ultimate confrontation with Satan. He initiated fasting as a regulation that was intertwined with prayer, and that would be required of His disciples (followers), of which we as His Queens are a part. First century believers and followers of God fasted to get ready for major events, therefore we cannot be exempt. Acts 13: 2-3 = *"While they were serving the Lord and fasting, the Holy Spirit said, "set apart for me Barnabas and Saul (Paul) for the work to which I have called them." Then after fasting and praying, they laid their hands on them [in approval and dedication] and sent them away [on their first journey].*

Acts 14:23 = *"When they had appointed elders for them in every church, having prayed with fasting, they entrusted them to the Lord in whom they believed [and joyfully accepted as the Messiah]."*

Fasting, in and of itself, does not move God to action, however, what does move God is when we dedicate ourselves to prayer while fasting. This type of sacrifice entails putting our undivided attention on God and yielding our entire body to Him. Esther knew she would need assistance in going before the king on behalf of her people, and this would necessitate fasting and praying. Usually a fast would require not eating from sunrise to sunset, but Esther asked for no eating or drinking for three days and three nights declaring *"Go gather all the Jews that are present in Susa, and observe a fast for me; do not eat or drink for three days, night or day. I and my maids also will fast in the same way. Then I will go in to [see] the king [without being summoned], which is against the law; and if I perish I perish."* (Esther 4:16). Though the Esther narrative does not mention prayer, it usually occurs concurrently with fasting in the Old Testament. This specific call to fast and pray would require rejection of individual needs and the comforts of life, to give undivided attention to God, in an effort to pay attention to Him and be obedient to His instructions. This went way beyond just Mordecai's and Esther's perceptions, and into the very core of who her heavenly King was and what He required. She had to listen carefully to hear Him so she could obey His words. Though God had brought Esther to the position in history where she could actually bring ultimate change, the choice of whether or not to obey was still hers to make.

My sister Queens, God has brought us to a place in time where we can make a difference in the church and in the world, but in order to know exactly what He requires of us and get our marching papers, we must fast and pray. We have been called to a divine appointment with the King that is not about us, but about our service to the Almighty King. Just as Esther's call was not so much about her being a Queen on the throne of Persia, neither is whatever we are called to always about the roles we play as Queens in the church. Sometimes God wants to take us higher and deeper and this re- quires speaking and listening to Him in a way that we don't normally do.

Usually at the beginning of each year the church calls a fast. This special time of fasting and prayer is done collectively, but should have a deeper impact on us individually. The problem is that oftentimes we conduct this season of consecration as a ritual and in obedience to our earthly leaders, without recognizing that this is how we receive our marching papers from the King about our new anointing for the year.

As I pen this section of the book it is the beginning of another year. I wanted to begin fasting and praying on day one of the year, but just couldn't get myself to adhere to it. As I went outside for my morning walk and prayer time with the King today, the third day of the New Year, I could feel the presence of the Holy Spirit nudging me to set myself in a place of consecration, because there is a new anointing awaiting me that require being completely set apart. The Royal Scepter has been put forth inviting me into the banquet hall of the King to receive my marching papers for the year. This is a set time for this Queen and my ears have to be attuned to receive my specific orders for the journey ahead. It is so much easier to be in this consecration collectively as a church, but when God wants you to do a specific thing He calls you out individually, just like He did with Queen Esther.

As Queens who have been given the regenerated birth of salvation, we must recognize, as stated repeatedly in this book, there is a specific calling for each one of us to do a specific thing in the Kingdom. For some of us the call is to be in the outer court of the Kingdom (the pews) and for others it is a frontline call to be in the inner court (the pulpit) or some other front line role. Regardless of where we will serve out our Queenly anointing, in order to receive a specific rhema word about it, we sometimes have to go the extra mile of emptying ourselves through a cleansing fast, combined with daily prayer. This is a time of completely giving ourselves to the Lord. This is a time of consecrating ourselves to the King. During this season we get the opportunity to hear from the King in ways that cut to the depth of our being, which aligns us to His personal plan as we incorporate the reading of His word in our daily regimen. This special time of consecration gives us the sense of boldness that

Esther acquired in her effort to complete the task for which she was sent into the royal palace to accomplish.

Consecration Scriptures:

Romans 12:1 = *"Therefore I urge you, brothers and sisters, by the mercies of God, to present your bodies [dedicating all of yourselves, set apart] as a living sacrifice, holy and well-pleasing to God, which is your rational (logical, intelligent) act of worship."*

As we embark on our fasting and prayer time as Queens, it seems only right to start with this dedicatory verse. We must begin with a sacrificial dedication of our bodies to the King. The prayer here would go something like this:

Dear Lord and King, I thank you for the gift of eternal life through the regeneration of salvation. I dedicate my entire body, inside and out, in service to you. I ask you to set me apart for your service in the Kingdom. I realize that in offering this part of me, I am now in your control to do what you will. I am no longer my own, but I belong to you and I seek to do whatever you desire, even when it doesn't line up with what I desire for myself. Your faithful and loving Queen _____ (Fill in the blank with your name).

1 Corinthians 6:19-20 = *"Do you not know that your body is a temple of the Holy Spirit who is within you, whom you have [received as a gift] from God, and that you are not your own [property]? 20 You were bought with a price [you were actually purchased with the precious blood of Jesus and made His own]. So then, honor and glorify God with your body."*

Recognizing that as Queens, our bodies are temples, it is only right that we rededicate them to the King. A great sacrificial price has been paid on our behalf on the cross; therefore we don't belong to ourselves. The prayer here would go something like this:

Dear Lord and King, I realize that my body is just as sacred to you as the physical temple built with bricks, and you don't force me to do anything I don't want to do. In recognizing how sacred this body is to you, I wholeheartedly and selflessly give myself to you. I enter into intimate prayer and fellowship with you so you can set me apart for whatever your plan is for me. I honor and glorify you with my body today. Your faithful and loving Queen_____

_____ (Fill in the blank with your name).

Joshua 3:5 = *"Then Joshua said to the people, "Sanctify yourselves [for His purpose], for tomorrow the LORD will do wonders (miracles) among you."*

As Queens, we must recognize, like the children of Israel, that we must consecrate ourselves for special use. God has something extremely special in store for our tomorrows that only we can accomplish individually, but we must be set apart. The prayer here would go something like this:

Dear Lord and King, I know there is something specific you have for me to do in this set time and it requires a season of praying and fasting. I know you have a purpose for me in this season and in order to embrace the Queenly anointing required for this plan; I must go into a season of seclusion with you so I can hear your voice more clearly. Therefore, I set my face like flint before you so I can get my marching orders. Your faithful and loving Queen

_____ (Fill in the blank with your name).

Jeremiah 29:11-13 = *"For I know the plans and thoughts that I have for you,' says the LORD, 'plans for peace and well-being and not for disaster, to give you a future and a hope. 12 Then you will call on me and you will come and pray to me, and I will hear [your voice] and I will listen to you. 13 Then [with a deep longing] you will seek me and require me [as a vital necessity] and [you will] find me when you search for me with all your heart."*

There is a future plan that the King has for each one of His Queens and though it sometimes seems bumpy on the journey, the plan is not to bring us harm, but to give us a future filled with hope. The requirement for understanding the plan is to seek the King with all our hearts. The prayer here would go something like this:

Dear Lord and King, though the journey seems extremely rough at times, I know your plan is not to hurt me, but that there is a futuristic plan to give me hope. I know that my Queenly duties in the Kingdom rely on me searching diligently for you and I can only do that during seasons of consecration. There is a deep longing in my heart to know your voice and know you better and this only comes through prayer and fasting. Help me oh King. Your faithful and loving Queen _____ (Fill in the blank with your name).

Psalm 91:1-2 = *"He who dwells in the shelter of the Most High Will remain secure and rest in the shadow of the Almighty [whose power no enemy can withstand]. I will say of the LORD, "He is my refuge and my fortress, My God, in whom I trust [with great confidence, and on whom I rely]!"*

Our Queenly anointing requires that we stay in the secret place with our King so He can entrust us with His secret things. It is only during seasons of prayer and fasting that we gain access to that most secret place with Him so we can be consecrated as the secret service agents He desires us to be in His Kingdom. The prayer here would go something like this:

Dear Lord and King, I seek to gain access to you in your secret place, which is also where I find refuge and security under your wings. I pray that you would embrace me during this season of consecration, so I will be ready for whatever you would have me to accomplish. I pray that you strengthen my confidence and trust in you to receive your commands for my life and walk with you without

fear. Your faithful and loving Queen _____
(Fill in the blank with your name).

It is obvious from these scriptures that our King wants to have special encounters with us so He can declare and decree His enormous plans for us. We, as Queens, must remain resolute in our quest for Him through prayer and fasting, so we are not deafened by the outside forces that want to keep us stagnant in our journey. We must, like Queen Esther, set strategic times to fast and pray, so we can walk circumspectly in the way of our King; gain spiritual growth; give the King the opportunity to work in and through us; and take pleasure in the blessings of salvation in the Kingdom.

I am Thine Oh Lord

I am Thine, O Lord, I have heard Thy voice,
And it told Thy love to me;
But I long to rise in the arms of faith,
And be closer drawn to Thee.

Draw me nearer, nearer, nearer blessed Lord,
To the cross where Thou hast died;
Draw me nearer, nearer, nearer, nearer blessed Lord,
To Thy precious, bleeding side.

Consecrate me now to Thy service, Lord,
By the power of grace divine;
Let my soul look up with a steadfast hope,
And my will be lost in Thine.

O the pure delight of a single hour
That before Thy throne I spend,
When I kneel in prayer, and with Thee, my God,
I commune as friend with friend!

There are depths of love that I yet may know
Ere Thee face to face I see;

There are heights of joy that I yet may reach
Ere I rest in peace with Thee.

How are you consecrating yourself for the great things the
King is about to do in your life, on this side of heaven?
****

Notes

My First Queenly Banquet

The scene opens with Esther being welcomed to meet with the king, though she was not officially invited. I can only imagine the knots that were in her stomach and throat as she thought about the petition she was about to make of the king. She was not sure how this request would be received, but she knew if she didn't make the request her people would perish. The narrative explained that she was dressed in her royal accoutrements, which more than likely made her even more beautiful than she already was. These royal garments supplemented her already beautiful exterior, making her even more precious to the king and worthy to meet with him without an invitation. As she entered the room she must have won his instant approval and favor, therefore, avoiding death.

Then Esther replied, "My petition and my request is this: 8 if I have found favor in the sight of the king, and if it pleases the king to grant my petition and to do as I request, may the king and Haman come to the banquet that I will prepare for them; and tomorrow I will do as the king says [and express my request]." (Esther 5:7-8)

Esther knew why she was there, but she also knew that her allegations would be a detriment to the king's highest official, Haman. She, thus, requested a more private setting than the open court to deliberate with the king and his official. However, she also knew the great importance placed on feasts in the Persian culture;

and that the guests would be obviously disposed to comply with the desires of the one hosting the event. Therefore, though it would mean having to schedule yet another meeting with the king, she knew that her heavenly King had set the stage for this most eventful moment and therefore, would grant her favor on all counts. The stage was set, not by Esther or even Mordecai, but by the King of all kings and she was ready.

We must always keep in mind that Haman represents a picture of Satan (the accuser of the brethren), the flesh and fleshly ways; therefore, his narcissistic attitude in this portion of the narrative should not be surprising. As he boasted about what he thought was about to happen, and how privileged he would be to be the only one invited to sit at Queen Esther's banquet along with the king, those around him listened intently. He spoke of his wealth and status in the same voice that he spoke of his hatred for Mordecai and the Jews. When the flesh raises its head we must be conscious of the fact that whatever is coming behind it can only be something wicked and evil. The profane counsel of Haman's wife and cohorts would lead to his detriment. The gallows he had built to inevitably kill Mordecai, was the same weapon that would be used in his demise. This is just a picture of how Satan utilizes our flesh while we are trying to live as Queens, to wreak havoc in our lives. Though Esther was taking a stand and knew exactly what she had to do, the enemy was in the background doing everything to thwart the plan of the Queen.

Regardless of what Haman was trying to do in the background, Esther remained unstoppable in her pursuit to defeat him and it would all come to a screeching halt at the banqueting table with the king. That night the king would be restless, like he probably had been before, but this session of insomnia was God ordained. Haman was also seemingly restless as he found himself in the king's court at a very unusual time of night. This was all working together to accomplish God's plan for Esther's initial anointing as Queen. Romans 8:28 is clearly exhibited in this part of the story: *"And we know [with great confidence] that God [who is deeply concerned about us] causes all things to work together [as a plan] for good for those who love God, to those who are called according to His plan and purpose."* God's plan was set and it could not be aborted.

Like Esther, there is a banqueting table experience that we too as Queens will encounter as we make our way to the promise. There is a certain level of preparation that is expected as we get ready to meet with the King. We too must be decked in our best jewels and attire to encounter His presence. Esther, though she was ready, had to wait for the set God inspired time that would lead to the freedom of a nation. God has ordained a set time for us as His Queens to perform great exploits, but there is a waiting process. It is during that waiting process that our Haman rises to the occasion to set a trap for our demise. We have to remember that prior to Esther becoming Queen she wore many disqualifying labels such as "orphan", "peasant", "slave" and "outsider". All these labels were to render her unfit to be a Queen. They were like scarlet letters written on her chest to hinder her from her destination to the banqueting table.

As I pen the pages of this manuscript, though not a biography, I can't help but think of my own scarlet letters hanging on my chest as tools of Haman (Satan) to abort my assignment as a Queen. However, I must choose, every day to adorn myself with my Queenly apparels and sup with the King at His table. In Matthew 5:14 Jesus referred to the disciples as the "light of the world", and at that point they had not yet begun to shine. God wants His

Queens to shine; however, He knows the oppositions we sometimes have to face that seek to tarnish our glow. Regardless of the many setbacks we encounter we must adorn ourselves in our royal robes and sit before the King each day, rebuking Haman (Satan) and his cohorts.

If you are anything like me you might be wondering if we are the light of the world, why does it seem so dark sometimes. You might be thinking, how come I am a Queen when life makes me feel like a peasant sometimes. If I am a Queen, where are all my jewels, how come my crown is tarnished and why am I being treated like a doormat? The answer to that and so many questions is basically defined by the gallows that Haman (Satan) has conspired to set, in an effort to steal, kill and totally destroy God's Queens.

My dear Queens, regardless of what it looks like, there is a banqueting table set in your honor, and the King is waiting for you to enter, fully clothed in your royal attire. How magnificent is it, the King is waiting with bated breath to meet with us every day. The table is always set for a special banquet, but the King is a gentleman and will not force us to sit and dine with Him. Therefore, like our Esther example we must take the initiative to request a banquet with Him. We will never be declined an appointment with our heavenly King, but we must take advantage of every available moment, even when Haman (Satan) tries to dialogue with us and make our lives a living hell. I sought ten scriptures (ten being a number of completion), that depict the Messianic banquet that we must look forward to everyday. These verses explicitly let us know the Lord our King has set the table and is waiting for us to sit and dine.

Isaiah 25:6 = *"On this mountain [Zion] the* LORD *of hosts will prepare a lavish banquet for all peoples [to welcome His reign on earth], A banquet of aged wines—choice pieces [flavored] with marrow, of refined, aged wines.*

Mount Zion refers to the future residence of the King and His Queens from everywhere. There is a feast being set on our behalf, where only royalty can sit to drink and eat the best of everything.

Luke 14:15 = *"When one of those who were reclining at the table with Him heard this, he said to Him, "Blessed (happy, prosperous, to be admired) is he who will eat bread in the kingdom of God!""*

Though many of us will not be the most likely candidates to be Queens, we are exactly who the King is looking for to sup with. Therefore, we should not hesitate to enter the banqueting hall because we feel worthless, because the King calls us His priceless daughters.

Psalm 23:5 = *"You prepare a table before me in the presence of my enemies. You have anointed and refreshed my head with oil; my cup overflows.*

Haman (Satan) the deceiver will always have a plot going on to destroy our Queenly anointing. However, a banquet table has been set for us that overflow so that we will lack nothing.

Joel 2:24-26 = *And the threshing floors shall be full of grain, And the vats shall overflow with new wine and oil. "And I will compensate you for the years that the swarming locust has eaten, the creeping locust, the stripping locust, and the gnawing locust—my great army which I sent among you. "You will have plenty to eat and be satisfied and praise the name of the LORD your God Who has dealt wondrously with you; And My people shall never be put to shame.*

As Queens we are promised that, although we may have squandered years in being disobedient like the children of Israel, the banqueting table is set and we are assured full restoration as a result of the grace and mercy of our King.

Isaiah 58:11 = *And the LORD will continually guide you, And satisfy your soul in scorched and dry places, And give strength to your bones; And you will be like a watered garden, And like a spring of water whose waters do not fail.*

When Queens request a banquet with the King and we keep our appointments by being obedient, we are promised an abundance of blessings and greater restoration in the future.

Revelation 7:16-17 = *They will hunger no longer, nor thirst anymore; nor will the sun beat down on them, nor any [scorching] heat; 17 for the Lamb who is in the center of the throne will be their Shepherd, and He will guide them to springs of the waters of life; and God will wipe every tear from their eyes [giving them eternal comfort]."*

At our banquet with the King we are promised complete and final release from Haman (Satan). Our King will embrace us and remove from our memory anything the enemy used to cause us suffering and pain.

Matthew 22:2 = *"The kingdom of heaven may be compared to a king who gave a wedding feast for his son.*

Our banquet with the King is likened to a wedding banquet where all are invited. However, this divine invitation is only for the chosen Queens who obey the commands of the King.

Revelation 19:7-9 = *"Let us rejoice and shout for joy! Let us give Him glory and honor, for the marriage of the Lamb has come [at last] and His bride (the redeemed) has prepared herself." 8 She has been permitted to dress in fine linen, dazzling white and clean—for the fine linen signifies the righteous acts of the saints [the ethical conduct, personal integrity, moral courage, and godly character of believers]. 9 Then the angel said to me, "Write, Blessed are those who are invited to the marriage supper of the Lamb.'" And he said to me [further], "These are the true and exact words of God."*

As Queens, it is such an honor to be invited to the banquet table of our King. Just as Esther was adorned in her fine Queenly at- tire, we too are expected to adorn and prepare ourselves for our sit down feast with the King of kings. We are His royal subjects and the royal table has been set, and we must dazzle Him with our lifestyles and Godly character, regardless of what Haman (Satan) has set as traps for us along the way.

Psalm 107:8-9 = *"Let them give thanks to the LORD for His lovingkindness, And for His wonderful acts to the children of men! ⁹ For He satisfies the parched throat, and fills the hungry appetite with what is good.*

Real satisfaction for God's Queens can be found, not in the physical food at the banqueting table, or in the material wealth gained in the palace, but only in gratifying the King's purpose for our lives.

The King's Table by Erin Lamb (Inspired by Jesus)

My Bride, My Love.
I've invited you to a continual feast at My table.
To dine with Me.
To meet with Me.
To be with Me.
My Beloved.
The one I gave my life for.

I made you for me.
You are of an elegant design.
Handcrafted.
An original masterpiece.
I see great beauty when I look into your heart.
I see a treasure.
Made for Me.

I love you with an everlasting love.
It is a love that existed before you.
And it will continue on into eternity.
I am rejoicing over you.
Singing you love songs.
Songs the Angels also sing.

My Bride My love.
I have prepared a place for us.
Here in Paradise.
Where the radiance of My Father,
Fills every crevice with His brilliance and beauty.

I have prepared a table for us.
It is decadent.
I ask that you come away…
Be with Me.
Come away with Me.

Lay aside the troubles of today.
Come feast at the Banquet Table.
My heart erupts with joy,
When you look My way,
When you seek My face.

I am overflowing with love for you.
I am relentlessly pursuing you to love you.
I am moving mountains for you that you cannot see.
I am praying for you continuously.
I gave My life so you and I could be,
Closer,
One,
Together for all eternity.

Here I am My beloved,
Desiring you,
Loving you,
Craving more profound intimacy.
I long for you to know Me.
Truly experience all that I am.

I long for you to be with Me.
I don't take My eyes off you.
You are covered in My Robe of Righteousness.
I gave you My name.
I sealed our covenant with My blood.

Eternal love,
It's what I pursued you for,
No human being can love you more.
No human being can fill your voids.

It is I who completes,
Who fills to overflowing.
Come drink of My cup and you will not thirst.
Come feast of My bread and you will hunger no more.

Come rest your head on My chest.
Feel My heart beat.
Can you hear it pounding?
It's a sweet melody.
My love for you is custom to you.

I know everything there is to know about you.
And I am offering you all of Me.
Come My love...
Come...
My Beloved, My Bride, My Love...
Come and feast with Me.
You are all so deeply loved.

How are you preparing for your banquet with the King?

****

Notes

A Providence of Hope

Though vindictive Haman had seemingly convinced the king that killing all the Jews in his kingdom was a good idea, God offered a providence of hope through Queen Esther. As we have seen throughout the narrative, Mordecai has convinced Esther to go in to the king and even though it meant the possibility of her demise, she agreed to the challenge. The most exhilarating scene occurred as Esther made her way through the king's court. We can only imagine how nervous she was, not knowing if she would be accepted, or killed for her efforts. However, the king's scepter was extended as a symbol that she was allowed to enter though uninvited. In essence, she had found favor with the king and this one action would bring ultimate hope for the Jewish nation.

As Queens in the Kingdom of God, we are offered salvation when He extends His scepter, allowing us to enter His royal court. Though coming face to face with Him should mean ultimate death, we are granted entrance to His throne room by means of the Holy Spirit. This was illustrated by the encounter Esther had with the earthly king of Persia. According to the law of that day, no one could enter the palace without being invited, so Esther was taking a risk (the biggest risk of her life). My dear Queens, we cannot enter the royal palace of our Redeeming King without His grace in pardoning our sins and bidding us a meeting through His Son Jesus, who allows us to draw near boldly.

Both Esther's encounter and ours require boldness, but in the end has the ability to provide hope for a generation of people. Just as the earthly king of Persia offered Esther up to half of the kingdom, God has offered the Queens in His royal court greatness beyond measure. The Bible says in Ephesians 3:20: *"Now to Him who is able to [carry out His purpose and] do superabundantly more than all that we dare ask or think [infinitely beyond our greatest prayers, hopes, or dreams], according to His power that is at work within us, 21 to Him be the glory in the church and in Christ Jesus throughout all generations forever and ever. Amen."* Our King gives us the ability to accomplish above and beyond what we could ask think or imagine, and the ability to bring providential hope to those around us who need a Savior.

We have been given a message to bring providential hope to a nation and it requires a level of boldness on the part of every Queen. It requires that we stay at the feet of our King and at times bowing our face to the ground on behalf of family, friends and even our nation. However, because the task seems so difficult we settle into our comfort zone with blinders on so we don't have to be chosen for the task of going to the King. Singer Tamela Mann sings a song called "Take Me to the King" and part of the lyrics says:

Take me to the King
I don't have much to bring
my heart is torn in pieces
It's my offering
Take me to the king

Truth is I'm tired
Options are few
I'm trying to pray
but where are you?
I'm all churched out

A Providence of Hope

**Hurt and abused
I can't fake
what's left to do?**

This powerful song speaks volumes about our Queenly journey, in that we recognize, though we don't have much to bring we are beckoned to come into the throne room of the King and sometimes we have to crawl on our bellies to get there. Sometimes we are not even absolutely sure if He is hearing our pleas, but we go anyway hoping to see His royal scepter set before us, offering anything in His Kingdom plan and purpose for our lives. In order for us to get our orders from the King we must step outside of our comfort zone, with Haman (Satan) at our heels waiting to trip us up. However, our prize is a nation waiting for hope that only our King can bring. The problem is we don't put our trust in Him to accomplish what He says He will through us. Esther had to believe with all her heart that her heavenly King would be with her as she entered the court of the earthly king. She was about to expose Haman, the king's right hand man and this required courage. As Queens, we too must be courageous enough to expose our Haman (Satan) for his schemes against us and the entire world.

The ammunition that Esther had at her disposal to destroy Haman was Mordecai's report of a planned assassination of the king. This report would win her ultimate favor with the king and destroy wicked Haman once and for all. Our ammunition to win favor with our King and ultimately destroy Satan is our providential hope of eternal life with our King. God's providential care for His Queens is the hallmark for supporting and directing us. He arranges the events of our life to accomplish His plan for us and Psalm 16:9-11 says *"Therefore my heart is glad and my glory [my innermost self] rejoices; My body too will dwell [confidently] in safety, ¹⁰For You will not abandon me* *to Sheol (the nether world, the place of the dead), Nor will You allow Your Holy One to undergo decay. 11 You will show me the path of life; In Your presence is fullness of joy; In Your right hand there are pleasures forevermore."* Nothing can overpower God. His providential care and hope lets us know the good, bad and even ugly in our lives cannot alter His ultimate plan to care for His Queens. In the midst of whatever situations we find ourselves, we as His Queens need to just wait for our time of rescue, because God has promised that good will come out of all of it (Romans 8:28). We can be comforted by the fact that He never works against us but always works for us. We can hold fast to Romans 8:31-32 which declares *"What then shall we say to all these things? If God is for us, who can be [successful] against us? 32 He who did not spare [even] His own Son, but gave Him up for us all, how will He not also, along with Him, graciously give us all things?"* Hardships will invade our space, sometimes in the same vein with blessings, but nothing happens to His Queens without His consent, since He knows what's best for us. In Esther's situation God's providential hope and care was obvious, though His name is mentioned no- where in the book. His reason for her becoming Queen had nothing to do with earthly royalty, but only His providential care for His people.

Likewise, God has a providential plan for each of His Queens that He is fulfilling right at this very moment. All we have to do is stand still and be quiet so we can hear the plan and obey without question. Though Satan's plan is always to steal, kill and destroy, our King's grace is always sufficient. We must keep in mind that a gallows has been set for Satan that will destroy him once and for all and save a nation of Queens from destruction. According to Revelation 12:9 *"And the great dragon was thrown down, the age-old serpent who is called the devil and Satan, he who continually deceives and seduces the entire inhabited world; he was thrown down to the earth, and his angels were thrown down with him."* Just as Haman, the enemy of the Jews, was hung on a gallows and destroyed, so Satan, the enemy of God's Queens will be destroyed. Our role in the Kingdom in the meantime is to continue our royal duties, which sometimes requires bold courageous acts to get Haman (Satan) off our heels and instead under our feet. While we wait for our enemy to be destroyed we must bask in the court of our King, who continuously gives us instructions for life from His Word.

Isaiah 50:2 = *"Why, when I came, was there no man [to greet me]? When I called, why was there no one to answer? Is my hand really so short that it cannot redeem [My servants]? Or have I no power to rescue? Listen carefully, with my rebuke I dry up the sea, I make the rivers into a desert; their fish stink because there is no water and die of thirst."*

It is obvious that God doesn't need our help; however, His Queens must remain diligent and obedient. The verse stipulates the fact that when God's Queens find themselves between a rock and a hard place, they sometimes seem to quiver in their boots, thinking the King is unable to save. He calls us to remembrance of the Red Sea experience of the Israelites, and the fact that His hand is not too short. He is still our God and we need not complain or fret, just stand still in His court, dressed in our royal attire and He will rescue.

1 Chronicles 29:11 = *"Yours, O LORD, is the greatness and the power and the glory and the victory and the majesty, indeed everything that is in the heavens and on the earth; Yours is the dominion and kingdom, O LORD, and You exalt Yourself as head over all."*

Though it may seem like our King sometimes forgets about us and leaves us hanging in mid-air, the scripture reminds us that our Lord and King (Yahweh if you please), has the Kingdom firmly in His grip. His Queens will come forth unscathed if we remember that He is exalted above all things in heaven and on earth. No ruler on earth or in hell is too big or powerful for our God to destroy. He says "hold fast my Queens, your King is in charge of all of it".

Job 1:21 = *"Naked (without possessions) I came [into this world] from* *my mother's womb, and naked I will return there. The* LORD *gave and the* LORD *has taken away; blessed be the name of the* LORD.*"

Sometimes God's Queens must suffer catastrophic losses in our tests on the journey. When our response is like Job's, the King gives us a passing grade for the tests we must go through as we peruse the royal court.

Isaiah 43:1 = "*But now, this is what the* LORD, *your Creator says, O Jacob, And He who formed you, O Israel, "Do not fear, for I have redeemed you [from captivity]; I have called you by name; you are Mine!*"

The Queens under God's regime must recognize that regardless of what we have done to disrupt our growth in the Kingdom, we have been redeemed and are now called into our royal lineage by our names. We belong to Him and no one can pluck us out of His hands.

Romans 8:28 = "*And we know [with great confidence] that God [who is deeply concerned about us] causes all things to work together [as a plan] for good for those who love God, to those who are called according to His plan and purpose.*"

God's desire is for good for all His Queens, therefore, even the bad things He can turn into good for us if we trust Him. The stipulation here is being called according to what God plans and purposes for us. Problems and crisis will not wreck what our King has in store for us. This good that He works out is only for those who accept Him as Savior and Lord of their lives.

Deuteronomy 8:3-4 = "*He humbled you and allowed you to be hungry and fed you with manna, [a substance] which you did not know, nor did your fathers know, so that He might make you understand [by personal experience] that man does not live by bread alone, but man lives by every word that proceeds out of the mouth of the* LORD. *⁴Your clothing did not wear out on you, nor did your feet swell these forty years.*"

God, in speaking to the children of Israel, is also speaking to

His Queens and lets us know that His providential care can be truly embraced when we humble ourselves before Him. The lives of His Queens can only be lived in abundance when we bask in His word with submissive hearts.

Psalm 3:2-6 = *Many are saying of me, "There is no help [no salvation] for him in God." Selah.³ but You, O LORD, are a shield for me, My glory [and my honor], and the One who lifts my head. ⁴ With my voice I was crying to the LORD, And He answered me from His holy mountain. Selah. ⁵ I lay down and slept [safely]; I awakened, for the LORD sustains me. ⁶ I will not be intimidated or afraid of the ten thousands who have set themselves against me all around.*

The great care that God has for His Queens is evident in the fact that He shields them from all that has the potential to bring them harm. He is with us even in the middle of the night when danger seems to be lurking, so we need not be threatened or fretful when life throws us curve balls, because it is just the King's way of alerting us to trust Him even more.

1 Corinthians 15:57-58 = *"but thanks be to God, who gives us the victory [as conquerors] through our Lord Jesus Christ. ⁵⁸ Therefore, my beloved brothers and sisters, be steadfast, immovable, always excelling in the work of the Lord [always doing your best and doing more than is needed], being continually aware that your labor [even to the point of exhaustion] in the Lord is not futile nor wasted [it is never without purpose]."*

The Queens of God remain champions even when outside forces try to infiltrate their territory. This requires being steadfast and unmovable when faced with all manner of adversity. There will be times of physical, emotional and spiritual exhaustion, but it is all a part of the Queenly anointing that we must walk in to get to our ultimate destination.

Psalm 147:11 = *"The LORD favors those who fear and worship Him [with awe-inspired reverence and obedience], those who wait for His mercy and loving-kindness."*

Queens are promised God's care on every terrain of life. Therefore, we must be determined in our worship and awe of the King. We are constantly being asked to wait, and it is in those times that we receive extensions to our wings that help us soar even higher than before.

The Invisible Hand: Coming to Grips with God's Providence by Ray Pritchard

He is in charge of:
What happens
When it happens
How it happens
Why it happens
And even what happens after it happens.

This is true of:
All events
In every place
From the beginning of time
He does this for our good and his glory.

He is not the author of sin, yet evil serves His purposes.
He does not violate our free will, yet free will serves His purposes.
We're not supposed to understand all this.
We're simply supposed to believe it.

How does knowing that as a Queen you are under God's providential care, make you respond differently to adversity?
****

136

Notes

_____

_____

_____

_____

_____

_____

_____

_____

_____

_____

_____

_____

_____

_____

_____

_____

_____

_____

_____

_____

The Plot Exposed

Esther had fasted and prayed as a result of disaster and insecurity, and already asked her people to fast and pray. Now she was ready to feast with the king. Esther did not wait for her deliverance to come; she prepared a feast in anticipation of her deliverance. She saw victory on the horizon and prepared this second feast in the presence of her husband, the king and her adversary, Haman. Esther had waited for her hour of emancipation and it was about to happen. Nothing can keep God's Queens from His omnipresence, His omniscience, His omnipotence and most importantly His unconditional love. Esther's beauty and demeanor granted her favor with the king and He again offered her whatever she desired in the kingdom.

Esther knew what she wanted, and though she probably quaked in her sandals, the words came flowing from her lips, *"If I have found favor in your sight, O king, and if it pleases the king, let my life be spared as my petition, and my people [be spared] as my request; 4 for we have been sold, I and my people, to be destroyed, killed and wiped out of existence."* (Esther 7:3-4a) These profound words must have sparked the king's attention as this disclosed who she was as a Jew. I can only imagine how Haman must have felt as he listened to the Queen state her case. He must have known his nasty scheme to steal, kill and destroy God's people was about to be exposed, and thus cause him destruction. However, Esther's clever scheme to have Haman at the banquet made it impossible for him to run and hide, which is most likely what he

139

wanted to do as he stood terrified before the king.

Esther finally exposed the plot for her life and the life of her people, after about five years as Queen. The question that would initiate Haman's final demise was *"Who is this, and where is the one who would devise such a scheme"?* WOW!!! Haman was trapped by his own schemes and what happened next was the ultimate reason for Esther becoming Queen. God had gone to great lengths to assure that His people would not perish and He used a Jewish orphan girl to accomplish the task. Though at this juncture of the narrative Haman would fall before Esther begging for his life, the king had other plans and his death sentence would be carried out. The gallows he built for the hanging ceremony he devised for Mordecai would become his own defeat. The Jewish nation would no longer remain powerless against their assailants, but under the king's new decree would be able to instigate the destruction of their enemies. Mordecai's emancipation as royalty would emanate from the courage of Esther, who he originally raised as his own daughter. She was not only a Queen in the earthly palace but would eventually take her rightful place with the King of all kings.

"Mordecai departed from the presence of the king in royal apparel of blue and white, with a large crown of gold and with a robe of fine linen and purple wool; and the city of Susa shouted and rejoiced. 16 For [at this time] the Jews had light [a dawn of new hope] and gladness and joy and honor. 17 in each and every province and in each and every city, wherever the king's command and his decree arrived, the Jews celebrated with gladness and joy, a feast and a holiday. And many among the peoples of the land became Jews, for the fear of the Jews [and their God] had fallen on them." (Esther 8:15-17)

Regardless of where we come from and how insignificant our

place in life seems, God's Queens have been anointed for such a time as this, and our anointing will ultimately lead to the destruction of our enemy Haman (Satan). 1 Peter 2:5 says *"You [believers], like living stones, are being built up into a spiritual house for a holy and dedicated priesthood, to offer spiritual sacrifices [that are] acceptable and pleasing to God through Jesus Christ."* God's Queens are being built up to connect with other Queens which is meant to result in us becoming a force to be reckoned with by the enemy. However, his clever schemes sometimes render us victims instead of victorious. Instead of choking in fear we must decipher what our role is in the Kingdom and surrender to the King.

If we are to walk in our roles as Queens and muster up enough courage to expose the plot of the enemy on our lives, we must first know and understand what our role is in the Kingdom. In 2 Timothy 2:20 Paul declares *"Now in a large house there are not only vessels and objects of gold and silver, but also vessels and objects of wood and of earthenware, and some are for honorable (noble, good) use and some for dishonorable (ignoble, common)."* I suppose we must first determine if we want to be honorable or dishonorable objects in the house of God.

Our minds are battlefields that Satan seeks to use as trampolines that he can trample on a whim. He comes against us with all the forces of hell because his plot is always to steal, kill and destroy God's beautiful Queens. Sometimes the attacks become so fierce we can't seem to muster enough energy to fight back. However, my Queenly sisters we can fight back, but only through the strength of our King, which means constant banquet meetings with Him to ac- quire our battle plan. He has given us every strategy in the pages of His divine manuscript, but if we never read it we become ill equipped to fight. All wise Queens know what to do to wrestle through the fight and get to the next day or sometimes even the next minute. One writer, though not referring to God's Queens, was firm about how we as believers should view the enemy of our souls (Satan). I utilized McDaniel (2015) analogy to strengthen my resolve about how we as Queens can expose Satan's schemes and win in his plot against us.

Queens must recognize their enemy:

Esther was well aware of whom her enemy was and she kept him close by so she could beat him at his own game. If we don't know who the real enemy of our soul is then chances are we won't win in the day to day battles of life. My Queenly sisters, we must know the schemes of our enemy recognize his skirmish strategies, be acquainted with his weak points and his powers. We have to be familiar with how he looks, and the masks he wears. This requires a shrewd awareness that only comes when we are in constant communication with the King. Frequently in our daily schedules, we get lost in our routines and lose sight of who the enemy really is. The end result is we fight against each other, our families, our friends and even the church—Satan laughs in those instances, because we become powerless and he wins. However, my Queenly sisters God's word reminds us in Ephesians 6:12 *"For our struggle is not against flesh and blood [contending only with physical opponents], but against the rulers, against the powers, against the world forces of this [present] darkness, against the spiritual forces of wickedness in the heavenly (supernatural) places."* The devil is very real and he desires to strip us of our Queenly anointing. His desire is for us to be unsuccessful; he desires for us to shrivel up and die; he wants us to be totally useless. In essence he wants to steal, kill, and destroy God's Queens. However, when we recognize him we can see him coming and utilize the King's strategies to destroy his plot.

God's Queens must know how Satan looks and what his job entails:

Accuser = Revelation 12:10 *"Then I heard a loud voice in heaven, saying, "Now the salvation, and the power, and the kingdom (dominion, reign) of our God, and the authority of His Christ have come; for the accuser of our [believing] brothers and sisters has been thrown down [at last], he who accuses them and keeps bringing charges [of sinful behavior] against them before our God day and night."*

Liar = John 8:44 *"You are of your father the devil, and it is your will to practice the desires [which are characteristic] of your father. He was a murderer from the beginning, and does not stand in the truth because there is no truth in him. When he lies, he speaks what is natural to him, for he is a liar and the father of lies and half-truths."*

Genesis 3:1 *"Now the serpent was more crafty (subtle, skilled in deceit) than any living creature of the field which the LORD God had made. And the serpent (Satan) said to the woman, "Can it really be that God has said, 'You shall not eat from [ll]any tree of the garden'?"*

Thief = John 10:10 *"The thief comes only in order to steal and kill and destroy. I came that they may have and enjoy life, and have it in abundance [to the full, till it overflows]."*

Deceiver = Revelation 12:9 *"And the great dragon was thrown down, the age-old serpent who is called the devil and Satan, he who continually deceives and seduces the entire inhabited world; he was thrown down to the earth, and his angels were thrown down with him.*

Matthew 7:15 *"Beware of the false prophets, [teachers] who come to you dressed as sheep [appearing gentle and innocent], but inwardly are ravenous wolves."*

Angel of light disguise = 2 Corinthians 11:14 *"And no wonder, since Satan himself masquerades as an angel of light.*

Tempter = Matthew 4:3 *"And the tempter came and said to Him,*

"If You are the Son of God, command that these stones become bread."

Adversary = 1 Peter 5:8 *"Be sober [well balanced and self-disciplined], be alert and cautious at all times. That enemy of yours, the devil, prowls around like a roaring lion [fiercely hungry], seeking someone to devour."*

Crafty = Genesis 3:1-5 *"Now the serpent was more crafty (subtle, skilled in deceit) than any living creature of the field which the LORD God had made. And the serpent (Satan) said to the woman, "Can it really be that God has said, 'You shall not eat from any tree of the garden'?" 2 And the woman said to the serpent, "We may eat fruit from the trees of the garden, 3 except the fruit from the tree which is in the middle of the garden. God said, 'You shall not eat from it nor touch it, otherwise you will die.'" 4 but the serpent said to the woman, "You certainly will not die! 5 For God knows that on the day you eat from it your eyes will be opened [that is, you will have greater awareness], and you will be like God, knowing [the difference between] good and evil."*

Ephesians 6:11-12 *"Put on the full armor of God [for His precepts are like the splendid armor of a heavily-armed soldier], so that you may be able to [successfully] stand up against all the schemes and the strategies and the deceits of the devil. 12 For our struggle is not against flesh and blood [contending only with physical opponents]; but against the rulers; against the powers; against the world forces of this [present] darkness; against the spiritual forces of wickedness in the heavenly (supernatural) places."*

Hindrance = 1 Thessalonians 2:18 *"For we wanted to come to you—I, Paul, again and again [wanted to come], but Satan hindered us."*

Matthew 16:23 = *"But Jesus turned and said to Peter, "Get behind Me, Satan! You are a stumbling block to Me; for you are not setting your mind on things of God, but on things of man."*

Beelzebub = Matthew 12:23-24 *"And all the multitudes were amazed and said, "Could this be the Son of David? 24 Now when the Pharisees heard it they said, "This fellow does not cast out demons except by Beelzebub, the ruler of the demons."*

When God's Queens recognize the enemy by all his names the plot for their lives is exposed, rendering them equipped to fight and win.

God's Queens must foresee Satan's attacks

We must recognize Satan as a cruel opponent, when we're at our weakest and most vulnerable moment that is when he attacks most forceful. He attacks when we are off guard and not on the alert, because he knows that when things are going well we let our guard down and tend to disregard the king. My Queenly sisters even when we are having amazingly wonderful days, and we feel powerful, we must be conscious of the fact that sinister forces wrestle in opposition to us, in the spiritual realm where we are unable to see them. When we think we can handle it that is when Satan attacks and tries to beat us at our own game. We must always be completely aware that Satan is on the prowl wanting to devour us. We must recognize our own weaknesses and know we can only find real strength at the banqueting table with God alone, never in our own flesh. We can never underestimate the enemy of our souls. When we are making a difference in the kingdom of God, we become a force to be reckoned with. Therefore, if we as His Queens live like salt and light in this world, we must know we will be attacked. We must stay aware, and not be surprised when opposing forces try to stop our influence for Christ. Hold fast to the fact that those opposing forces cannot and will not win. God's Queens must not be afraid, because the Lord our God promises to fight for us.

God's Queens must protect themselves from Satan's schemes

Stay alert = 1 Peter 5:8 *"Be sober [well balanced and self-disciplined], be alert and cautious at all times. That enemy of yours, the devil, prowls around like a roaring lion [fiercely hungry], seeking someone to devour."*

Resist Satan = James 4:7 *"So submit to [the authority of] God. Resist the devil [stand firm against him] and he will flee from you."*

Know we are conquerors = Romans 8:37 *"Yet in all these things we are more than conquerors and gain an overwhelming victory through Him who loved us [so much that He died for us]."*

Take up our sword = Ephesians 6:17 *"And take THE HELMET OF SALVATION, and the sword of the Spirit, which is the Word of God.*

Know God is with us = Romans 16:20 *"The God of peace will soon crush Satan under your feet. The [wonderful] grace of our Lord Jesus be with you."*

Stand strong = Ephesians 6:10 *"In conclusion, be strong in the Lord [draw your strength from Him and be empowered through your union with Him] and in the power of His [boundless] might."*

It is obvious that God's Queens are under Satan's attack and that he desires to steal, kill and destroy us if he gets the chance. Like Esther, however, we need to keep our eyes on him and understand his strategy, so we can fight and win. Esther knew Haman (Satan) had a plot to destroy her and her people, so she concocted a scheme of her own to catch him at his own game. We must be tactical in beating Satan at his games that he utilizes to trick; cripple and ultimately destroy us. We must never underestimate the power of our enemy, thus prepare to win in the plot that he has devised for our downfall. It is amazing to me how very little we talk about Satan and his demonic forces, it is almost as if we ignore him in the hopes he will disappear, or we just don't think he exists at all. We must always remember that he is very real and once lived in heaven, therefore, he knows a lot more than we sometimes give him credit for. We need to invite him to the banqueting table with the King of kings, in an effort to expose his plots against us and begin the process of killing.

How are you exposing the plot that Satan has for your life? How has this impacted your anointing as a Queen?

****

Notes

_____

_____

_____

_____

_____

_____

_____

_____

_____

_____

_____

_____

_____

_____

_____

_____

_____

_____

_____

Promoted by God

There is a promotion in store for all God's Queens, and His desire is for us to endure to the end, regardless of how bleak it may look, and how insurmountable the hills may seem to climb. Esther's success was solely based on what God would do in her circumstances. The king had an array of women to choose from when he made Esther the successor to Vashti. The women who vied for the position alongside Esther were privy to all the adornments of the world to make them outwardly attractive to the king. Therefore, they were going to the king in their own strength, in an effort to win his favor. Esther, as a result of her humble demeanor, requested nothing, except what the king's eunuch offered as preparation for her meeting with his royal highness. Esther 2:17 explained: *"Now the king loved Esther more than all the other women, and she found favor and kindness with him more than all the [other] virgins, so that he set the royal crown on her head and made her queen in the place of Vashti."*

Esther didn't depend on her own efforts or the efforts of the world, but remained humble and God granted her favor. Her dependence on God, not only granted her unmerited favor with the earthly king, but also with her heavenly King. Esther's complete obedience saved God's people from genocide (being deliberately killed). The reality is she had no idea what would happen to her when she approached the king. She acted in full dependence on her heavenly King, and by doing so saved a nation and received the best promotion. Esther's divine moment of promotion came by accepting her responsibility to face the king. God will use us only if we are ready—or He will find someone else. If Esther had declined the invitation God would have promoted someone else. Therefore, we must be willing to stand in courage, even when it is not popular to do so, and risk everything to be promoted.

My dear Queens, we don't get a pass on this one, but we must daily ask ourselves who we are depending on for promotion. If we're honest we will admit that sometimes we depend on man and the world more than we depend on God. However, our heavenly King has the power to bring the Haman's in our life to a complete stand still. Therefore, we must embrace the power of the Holy Spirit in our lives, recognizing if we just turn our will over to our heavenly King, He will eventually promote us to unbelievable positions on this side of heaven, eventually leading to our ultimate promotion to heaven.

When you humble yourself and cease from your efforts to promote yourself, and depend on Jesus alone, the Lord Himself will be your promotion and increase. Like Esther, you will stand out in a crowd and obtain grace and favor with God and man. Also, because Esther was promoted to become the queen, she was in a favored position to protect all the Jewish people in the kingdom from being killed. When the Lord promotes you, He gives you the influence to be a blessing to the people around you. There are no coincidences, only God-incidents. The Lord will bless you to be a blessing (The Gospel of Grace, 2011, p. 1)

Our Queenly journey requires a great level of humility and a level of suffering, and no matter where or how promotion comes, we must realize it is only as a result of God's anointing and favor.

Once we submit to the anointing we must stand with courage, realizing this is where the real war begins in an effort to hinder our pro- motion. When we completely depend on Him we become great in the sight of the world, putting us in favored positions to accomplish great feats. We become Queens among everyone we encounter at home, church, work and beyond. The idea is to relinquish all our activities to the King of all kings and BE STILL.

Psalm 34:19-20 declares, *"Many hardships and perplexing circumstances confront the righteous, the Lord rescues him from them all. He keeps all his bones; not one of them is broken."* Many hardships and perplexing circumstances confront God's Queens, but the Lord has promised to rescue us from all of them. No matter how difficult it becomes we will not be broken, but come forth whole. God has ordained that His Queens must go through many hardships sometimes to embrace our anointing and enter His kingdom. He will deliver us from our hardships and grant us major promotions when his purpose for us has been accomplished (either by supernatural intervention in this life or victorious death that takes us to heaven where there is no suffering). To embrace our Queenly promotion we must put on our armor and be courageous and determined to fight. This requires being willing to give our lives for the cause of being anointed Queen and potentially being promoted.

As this book, dedicated to the Queens in the kingdom of God, comes to a close it would be inaccurate not to talk about scriptures pertaining to the amazing promotion to be acquired from God.

Genesis 12:2 = *"And I will make you a great nation, And I will bless you [abundantly], And make your name great (exalted, distinguished); And you shall be a blessing [a source of great good to others];"*

God promised to make Abraham a great nation and thus, pronounced an abundance of blessings on him and his descendants after him. These same blessings and promotions are promised to

His Queens, but the same requirement of complete obedience still stands. How are we walking in complete obedience?

Esther 6:11 = *"So Haman took the royal robe and the horse and dressed Mordecai, and led him on horseback through the open square of the city, proclaiming before him, "This is what shall be done for the man whom the king desires to honor."*

Though Haman planned to hang Mordecai on the gallows he built and wear the royal robes himself, God reversed the verdict and caused Haman disgrace by promoting Mordecai instead. God will cause the enemies of His Queens to help in their promotion process if they remain faithful. How are you remaining faithful in the kingdom work assigned to you?

Daniel 2:48 = *"Then the king promoted Daniel [to an exalted position] and gave him many great gifts, and he made him ruler over the entire province of Babylon and chief governor over all the wise men of Babylon."*

Daniel received promotion from the king who gave him honor as a result of God's favor. God's Queens have been afforded favor by God by those in high places, but only when we reverence Him in all we do. How are you showing reverence to God in those places of honor that He allows?

Daniel 3:30 = *"Then the king caused Shadrach, Meshach, and Abednego to prosper in the province of Babylon."*

Though these men had been deposed from their positions like Vashti, God allowed the king to reinstate them to those places of esteem. Though God's Queens may, at times, have to be deposed from their positions, God has the power to reinstate us when we aspire to follow Him in all we do. What has God done to reinstate you to a place from where you were once deposed?

1 Samuel 7:8 & 10 = *"And the sons of Israel said to Samuel, "Do not*

cease to cry out to the LORD *our God for us, so that He may save us from the hand of the Philistines. As Samuel was offering up the burnt offering, the Philistines approached for the battle against Israel. Then the* LORD *thundered with a great voice that day against the Philistines and threw them into confusion, and they were defeated and fled before Israel."*

God saved the children of Israel as a result of Samuel's intercession. He threw their oppressors into utter confusion which caused them victory. No matter what it looks like, God has our backs, causing those who bring us conflict to be confused causing us to win our battles, but prayer is the key. How are you seeking God in prayer concerning your battles?

Psalm 75:6-7 = *"For not from the east, nor from the west, nor from the desert comes exaltation. But God is the Judge; He puts down one and lifts up another."*

God is the creator of all and in control of all things; therefore, He has the power to promote or demote whoever He sees fit. The same demotion and promotion offered to Vashti and Esther belongs to God's Queens and we must be poised to move in whatever direction He chooses. How are you prepared for whatever God chooses for you?

Luke 1:52 = *"He has brought down rulers from their thrones, and exalted those who were humble."*

God has been instrumental in bringing down those who rule over His people just so He could exalt those He chooses. God will bring down whoever He desires to exalt His Queens but it requires humility. Who does God need to bring down in order to promote you? Are you prepared?

1 Peter 5:6-7 = *"Therefore humble yourselves under the mighty hand of God [set aside self-righteous pride], so that He may exalt you [to a place of honor in His service] at the appropriate time, 7 casting all your cares [all your anxieties, all your worries, and all your concerns, once and for all] on Him, for*

He cares about you [with the deepest affection, and watches over you very carefully].

What promotions have you been offered and how are you embracing them?

****

Notes

_____

_____

_____

_____

_____

_____

_____

_____

_____

_____

_____

_____

_____

_____

_____

_____

_____

_____

_____

_____

_____

_____

Conclusion

God uses everything and everybody in our lives for His divine purpose and plan in an effort to crown His Queens. Like Esther embraced Mordecai's counsel, we too must embrace the Holy Spirit's counsel so we can rise to the occasion to walk in our Queenly anointing. Hebrews 2:8 says it best; *"YOU HAVE PUT ALL THINGS IN SUBJECTION UNDER HIS FEET [confirming his supremacy]." Now in putting all things in subjection to man; He left nothing outside his control. But at present we do not yet see all things subjected to him.* No part of our lives is untouched. God is in control of every aspect, whether we want Him to be or not and there is nothing that is not subject to Him. The best thing His Queens can do is to search for and surrender to His will. **What is your purpose as Queen in the kingdom?** Being a Queen requires knowing your purpose. **What has God called you to do FOR SUCH A TIME AS THIS? Has circumstances hindered your destination?** It is time to step into your greatness and it requires you to be whole, not broken. 1 Peter 2:4-10 says:

"Come to Him [the risen Lord] as to a living Stone which men rejected and threw away, but which is choice and precious in the sight of God.⁵ You [believers], like living stones, are being built up into a spiritual house for a holy and dedicated priesthood, to offer spiritual sacrifices [that are] acceptable and pleasing to God through Jesus

Christ. [6] For this is contained in Scripture: "BEHOLD, I AM LAYING IN ZION A CHOSEN STONE, A PRECIOUS (honored) CORNERSTONE, AND HE WHO BELIEVES IN HIM [whoever adheres to, trusts in, and relies on Him] WILL NEVER BE DISAPPOINTED [in his expectations]." [7] This precious value, then, is for you who believe [in Him as God's only Son—the Source of salvation]; but for those who disbelieve,

"THE [very] STONE WHICH THE BUILDERS REJECTED HAS BECOME THE CHIEF CORNERSTONE," [8] and,

"A STONE OF STUMBLING AND A ROCK OF OFFENSE";

For they stumble because they disobey the word [of God], and to this they [who reject Him as Savior] were also appointed. [9] But you are A CHOSEN RACE, A royal PRIESTHOOD, A CONSECRATED NATION, A [special] PEOPLE FOR God's OWN POSSESSION, so that you may proclaim the excellencies [the wonderful deeds and virtues and perfections] of Him who called you out of darkness into His marvelous light. [10] Once you were NOT A PEOPLE [at all], but now you are GOD'S PEOPLE; once you had NOT RECEIVED MERCY, but now you have RECEIVED MERCY.

As you perused this, my most special book that I have penned so far, have you embraced your anointing as a Queen in the kingdom (A WOMAN OF GREATNESS)? If not, WHY NOT? First and foremost, have you submitted to the anointing by accepting Christ as your personal Savior? If not, WHY NOT? You cannot be a Queen unless you surrender to the initial calling of the King to be His daughter. Romans 10:9-10 declares:

If you acknowledge and confess with your mouth that Jesus is Lord [recognizing His power, authority, and majesty as God], and believe in your heart that God raised Him from the dead, you will be saved. [10] *For with the heart a person believes [in Christ as Savior] resulting in his justification [that is, being made righteous—being freed of the guilt of sin and made acceptable to God]; and with the mouth he acknowledges and confesses [his faith openly], resulting in and confirming [his] salvation.*

Before Esther could submit to her calling as Queen and go in to the king, she had to be prepared **(the initial preparation for us is to accept Christ as Savior). If you read this far in the book and still have not yet said yes to Christ in asking Him to be your personal Savior; my desire is that you pause right now and recite this prayer.**

Dear Lord,

I humbly bow before you, recognizing that without you in my heart and life, I cannot be a true Queen in your kingdom. You said in your word, if I confess with my mouth and believe in my heart that Jesus is Lord, I will be saved. Today I want to take this moment to make that confession of faith. I thank you that today _____(fill out the date) I_____(fill in your name) receive you by faith into my heart. I am saved, I am free and I am a QUEEN!!! In Jesus name I pray, AMEN!!!

A Prayer for the Queens

Dear Lord and loving Savior I pray for your Queens today, that they would take every opportunity to embrace their anointing as Queens. I pray especially for those who have not yet taken the first step to accepting you as Savior that they would say YES to your invitation to becoming Queens in your kingdom today. I pray for these special ladies that they would recognize who they truly are and not allow anything or anyone to deter them from being who you planned for them to be. Though much has happened to obstruct and delay their destiny, I pray that they would rise above those things and boldly approach your throne so you can greet them with your royal scepter. I pray that they would be resolute, admirable, purposeful, and determined and unwavering in allowing you to use them FOR SUCH A TIME AS THIS. I continuously pray that they would be healed, restored, delivered and blessed in this season as they courageously embrace their QUEENLY ANOINTING. In Jesus name AMEN!!!

I take this time to thank you for reading this God inspired manuscript that God allowed me to pen, as a love letter for His Queens. Though you may be going through some unbelievable things in your life right now, I believe it is only to strengthen you and cause you to trust your King even more. Set aside time to bask in those precious moments with your King, at His banqueting table, so He can expose you to who He really is and who He desires for you to be. Be firm in your stance to be a Queen, and He promises to promote you and grant you the desires of your heart. I promise He never goes back on His word and will bless you above and beyond what you can ask, think or imagine.

Your Sister and Fellow QUEEN,

Dr. Sharon

Queenly Questions to Think About

1. How is the story of Esther a metaphor for what we face in our Queenly roles?

2. Which Queen (Vashti or Esther) best describes where you are in your Queenly journey?

3. Who is the Mordecai in your life? How are you utilizing their words of wisdom to help you function in your anointing?

4. How has or is your Queenly anointing being crippled?

5. How will you use what you have learned in this book to reestablish your royal position?

6. Has brokenness disrupted your journey as a Queen? How?

7. What will it take to retrieve your crown?

8. Has this book given you any tools to help regain what you will need to walk as a Queen?

9. Are you embracing your anointing for such a time as this? How?

10. What are your thoughts concerning God as your ultimate King?

References

Angelou, M. (n. d.). Phenomenal Woman. *Poem Hunter.* Retrieved from https://www.poemhunter.com/poem/phenomenal-woman/

GotQuestions.org (n. d.). What does it mean to be anointed? Retrieved from https://www.gotquestions.org/anointed.html

Heller, R. T. (2003). Esther's hidden strength. *Purim.* Retrieved from http://www.aish.com/h/pur/t/dt/48953946.html

Lamb, E. (2015). *The King's table.* Retrieved from https://ithoughtiknewwhatlovewas.com/2015/09/17/the-kings-table-love-poem-for-the-bride-of-christ/

McDaniel, D. (2015). *How to expose the schemes of the enemy (and 6 ways to protect yourself).* Retrieved from https: //www.crosswalk.com/faith/spiritual-life/how-to-expose-the-schemes-of-the-enemy-and-6-ways-to-protect-yourself.html

Payne, S. L. (n. d.). *The anointing is on your life.* Retrieved from https://allpoetry.com/poem/2561086--The-Anointing-Is-On-Your-Life-by-suzzieque53

Pritchard, R. (1997). The invisible hand: Coming to grips with God's providence. *Keep Believing Ministries.* Retrieved from https://www.keepbelieving.com/sermon/1997-02-02-The-Invisible-Hand-Coming-to-Grips-With-Gods-Providence/

The Gospel of Grace (2011). How Esther obtained favor. *Being Part of the New Covenant.* Retrieved from https://beingunderthenewcovenant.wordpress.com/2011/08/18/how-esther-obtained-favor/

The Book of Esther

Esther Chapters 1-10 Amplified Bible (AMP)

The Banquets of the King (Chapter 1)

It was in the days of Ahasuerus (Xerxes) who reigned from India to Ethiopia (Cush) over 127 provinces, 2 in those days when King Ahasuerus sat on his royal throne which was at the citadel in Susa [the capital of the Persian Empire], 3 in the third year of his reign he held a banquet for all his officials and his attendants. The army *officers* of Persia and Media, the nobles and the officials of the provinces were there in his presence. 4 And he displayed the riches of his glorious kingdom and the splendor of his great majesty for many days, 180 days *in all.*

5 When these days were completed, the king held a banquet for all the people who were present at the citadel in Susa [the capital], from the greatest [in importance] to the least, a seven-day feast in the courtyard of the garden of the king's palace. 6 *There were curtains* (draperies) of fine white and violet linen fastened with cords of fine purple linen to silver rings and marble columns. The couches of gold and silver *rested* on a mosaic floor of porphyry, marble, mother-of-pearl, and precious *colored* stones. 7 Drinks were served in various kinds of golden goblets, and the royal wine was plentiful, in accordance with the generosity of the king. 8 The drinking was *carried on* in accordance with the law; no one was compelled [to drink], for the king had directed each official of his household to comply with each guest's wishes. 9 Queen Vashti also held a [separate] banquet for the women in the palace of King Ahasuerus.

Queen Vashti's Refusal

10 On the seventh day, when the king's heart was joyful with wine (in high spirits), he commanded Mehuman, Biztha, Harbona, Bigtha, Abagtha, Zethar, and Carkas, the seven eunuchs who served in the presence of King Ahasuerus [as his attendants], 11 to bring Queen Vashti before the king, wearing her royal crown (high turban), to display her beauty before the people and the officials, for she was lovely to see. 12 But Queen Vashti refused to come at the king's command, which was delivered [to her] by the eunuchs. So the king became extremely angry and burned with rage.

13 Then the king spoke to the wise men who understood the times [asking for their advice]—for it was the custom of the king *to speak* before all those who were familiar with law and legal matters— 14 and who were close to him [as advisors]: Carshena, Shethar, Admatha, Tarshish, Meres, Marsena, and Memucan, the seven officials of Persia and Media who had access to the king and were ranked highest in the kingdom. 15 [He said,] "According to the law, what is to be done with Queen Vashti because she did not obey the command of King Ahasuerus *which was conveyed* by the eunuchs?" 16 And Memucan answered in the presence of the king and the officials, "Vashti the queen has not only wronged the king but [also] all the officials (royal representatives) and all the peoples who are in all the provinces of King Ahasuerus. 17 For the queen's con- duct will become known to all women, causing them to look on their husbands with contempt (disrespect), since they will say, 'King Ahasuerus commanded Queen Vashti to be brought before him, but she did not come.' 18 This [very] day the ladies of Persia and Media who have heard of the queen's refusal will speak [in the same way] to all the king's officials, and there will be plenty of contempt and anger. 19 If it pleases the king, let a royal command be issued by

him and let it be written in the laws of the Persians and Medes so that it cannot be repealed *or* modified, that Vashti is no longer to come before King Ahasuerus; and let the king give her royal position to another who is better *and* more worthy than she. 20 So when the king's great decree is proclaimed throughout his [extensive] kingdom, all women will give honor to their husbands, from the great to the insignificant."

21 This statement (advice) pleased the king and the officials, and the king did what Memucan proposed. 22 So he sent letters to all the royal provinces, to each province in its own script and to each people in their own language, saying that every man should be the master *and* rule in his own home and that ⌐he should speak [in the household] in the language of his own people.

Vashti's Successor Sought (Chapter 2)

After these things, when the wrath of King Ahasuerus (Xerxes) had subsided, he remembered Vashti and what she had done and what had been decreed against her. 2 Then the king's attendants, who served him, said, "Let beautiful young virgins be sought for the king. 3 Let the king appoint administrators in all the provinces of his kingdom, and have them gather all the beautiful young virgins to the citadel in Susa, into the harem, under the custody of Hegai, the king's eunuch, who is in charge of the women; and let their beauty preparations be given *to them*. 4 Then let the young woman who pleases the king be queen in place of Vashti." This pleased the king, and he did accordingly.

5 There was a certain Jew in the citadel of Susa whose name was Mordecai the son of Jair, the son of Shimei, the son of Kish, a Benjamite, 6 who had been deported from Jerusalem with the captives who had been exiled with Jeconiah king of Judah, whom Nebuchadnezzar the king of Babylon had exiled. 7 He was the

guardian of Hadassah, that is Esther, his uncle's daughter, for she had no father or mother. The young woman was beautiful of form and face; and when her father and mother died, Mordecai took her in as his own daughter.

Esther Finds Favor

8 So it came about when the king's command and his decree were proclaimed and when many young women were gathered together in the citadel of Susa into the custody of Hegai, that Esther was taken to the king's palace [and placed] in the custody of Hegai, who was in charge of the women. 9 Now the young woman pleased Hegai and found favor with him. So he quickly provided her with beauty preparations and her [portion of] food, and he gave her seven choice maids from the king's palace; then he transferred her and her maids to the best *place* in the harem. 10 Esther did not reveal [the Jewish background of] her people or her family, for Mordecai had instructed her not to do so. 11 Every day Mordecai [who was an [i] attendant in the king's court] walked back and forth in front of the courtyard of the harem to learn how Esther was getting along and what was happening to her.

12 Now when it was each young woman's turn to go before King Ahasuerus, after the end of her twelve months under the regulations for the women—for the days of their beautification were completed as follows: six months with oil of myrrh and six months with [sweet] spices *and* perfumes and the beauty preparations for women— 13 then the young woman would go before the king in this way: anything that she wanted was given her to take with her from the harem into the king's palace. 14 In the evening she would go in and the next morning she would return to the second harem, to the

custody of Shaashgaz, the king's eunuch who was in charge of the concubines. She would not return to the king unless he delighted in her and she was summoned by name.

15 Now *as for* Esther, the daughter of Abihail the uncle of Mordecai who had taken her in as his [own] daughter, when her turn came to go in to the king, she requested nothing except what Hegai the king's eunuch [and attendant] who was in charge of the women, advised. And Esther found favor in the sight of all who saw her. 16 So Esther was taken to King Ahasuerus, to his royal palace in the tenth month, that is, the month of Tebeth (Dec-Jan), in the seventh year of his reign.

Esther Becomes Queen

17 Now the king loved Esther more than all the *other* women, and she found favor and kindness with him more than all the [other] virgins, so that he set the royal crown on her head and made her queen in the place of Vashti. 18 Then the king held a great banquet, Esther's banquet, for all his officials and his servants; and he made a festival for the provinces and gave gifts in accordance with the resources of the king.

19 And when the virgins were gathered together the second time, Mordecai [n]was sitting at the king's gate. 20 Esther had not revealed her family or her people [that is, her Jewish background], just as Mordecai had instructed her; for Esther did what Mordecai told her just as when she was under his care.

Mordecai Saves the King

21 In those days, while Mordecai was sitting at the king's gate, Bigthan and Teresh, two of the king's eunuchs who guarded the door, became angry and conspired to attack King Ahasuerus. 22 But

the plot became known to Mordecai, who informed Queen Esther, and Esther told the king in Mordecai's name. 23 Now when the plot was investigated and found *to be true*, both men were hanged on the gallows. And it was recorded in the Book of the Chronicles in the king's presence.

Haman's Plot against the Jews (Chapter 3)

After these things King Ahasuerus (Xerxes) promoted Haman, the son of Hammedatha the Agagite, and advanced him and established his authority over all the officials who were with him. 2 All the king's servants who were at the king's gate [in royal service] bowed down and honored *and* paid homage to Haman; for this is what the king had commanded in regard to him. But Mordecai [a Jew of the tribe of Benjamin] neither bowed down nor paid homage [to him]. 3 Then the king's servants who were at the king's gate said to Mordecai, "Why are you disregarding the king's command?" 4 Now it happened when they had spoken to him day after day and he would not listen to them, that they told Haman to see whether Mordecai's reason [for his behavior] would stand [as valid]; for he had told them that he was a Jew. 5 When Haman saw that Mordecai neither bowed down nor paid homage to him, he was furious. 6 But he disdained laying hands on Mordecai alone, for they had told him *who* the people of Mordecai were (his nationality); so Haman determined to destroy all the Jews, the people of Mordecai, who *lived* throughout the kingdom of Ahasuerus.

7 In the first month, the month of Nisan (Mar-Apr), in the twelfth year of King Ahasuerus, Haman cast Pur, that is, the lot, cast before him day after day [to find a lucky day to approach the king], month after month, until the twelfth month, the month of Adar (Feb-Mar). 8 Then Haman said to King Ahasuerus, "There is a

certain people scattered [abroad] and dispersed among the peoples in all the provinces of your kingdom; their laws are different from *those* of all *other* people, and they do not observe the king's laws. Therefore it is not in the king's interest to [tolerate them and] let them stay *here.* 9 If it pleases the king, let it be decreed that they be destroyed, and I will pay ten thousand talents of silver into the hands of those who carry out the *king's* business, to put into the king's treasuries." 10 Then the king removed his signet ring from his hand [that is, the special ring which was used to seal his letters] and gave it to Haman, the son of Hammedatha the Agagite, the enemy of the Jews. 11 The king said to Haman, "The silver is given to you and the people *also,* to do with them as you please."

12 Then the king's scribes (secretaries) were summoned on the thirteenth day of the first month, and it was written just as Haman commanded to the king's satraps (chief rulers), and to the governors who were over each province and to the officials of each people, each province according to its script (writing), each people according to their own language; being written in the name of King Ahasuerus and sealed with the king's signet ring. 13 Letters were sent by couriers to all the king's provinces to destroy, to kill and to annihilate all the Jews, both young and old, women and children, in one day, the thirteenth [day] of the twelfth month, which is the month of Adar (March 7, 473 B.C.), and to seize their belongings as plunder. 14 A copy of the edict to be decreed as law in every province was published to all the peoples, so that they would be ready for this day. 15 The couriers went out hurriedly by order of the king, and the decree was issued at the citadel in Susa. And while the king and Haman sat down to drink, the city of Susa was perplexed [by the unusual and alarming decree].

Esther Learns of Haman's Plot (Chapter 4)

Now when Mordecai learned of everything that had been done, he tore his clothes [in mourning], and put on sackcloth and ashes, and went out into the center of the city and cried out loudly and bitterly. 2 He went [only] as far as the king's gate, because no one was to enter the king's gate dressed in sackcloth. 3 In each and every province that the decree and law of the king reached, there was great mourning among the Jews, with fasting, weeping and wailing; and many lay on sackcloth and ashes.

4 When Esther's maids and her eunuchs came and told her [what had happened], the queen was seized by great fear. She sent garments to clothe Mordecai so that he would remove his sackcloth, but he did not accept them. 5 Then Esther summoned Hathach, one of the king's eunuchs, whom the king had appointed to attend her, and ordered him *to go* to Mordecai to find out what this issue was and why it had come about. 6 So Hathach went out to Mordecai in the [open] square of the city, which was in front of the king's gate. 7 Mordecai told him everything that had happened to him, and the exact amount of money that Haman had promised to pay to the king's treasuries for the destruction of the Jews. 8 Mordecai also gave him a copy of the text of the decree which had been issued in Susa for the Jews destruction, so that he might show Esther and explain it to her, and order her to go in to the king to seek his favor and plead with him for [the lives of] her people.

9 Hathach came back and told Esther what Mordecai had said. 10 Then Esther spoke to Hathach and ordered him *to reply* to Mordecai, saying: 11 "All the king's servants and the people of the king's provinces know that for any man or woman who comes to the king to the inner court without being summoned, he has but one law, that he is to be put to death, unless the king holds out to

him the golden scepter so that he may live. And as for me, I have not been summoned to come to the king for these [last] thirty days." 12 So they told Mordecai what Esther had said.

13 Then Mordecai told them to reply to Esther, "Do not imagine that you in the king's palace can escape any more than all the Jews. 14 For if you remain silent at this time, liberation and rescue will arise for the Jews from another place, and you and your father's house will perish [since you did not help when you had the chance]. And who knows whether you have attained royalty for such a time as this [and for this very purpose]?"

Esther Plans to Intercede

15 Then Esther told them to reply to Mordecai, 16 "Go, gather all the Jews that are present in Susa, and observe a fast for me; do not eat or drink for three days, night or day. I and my maids also will fast in the same way. Then I will go in to [see] the king [without being summoned], which is against the law; and if I perish, I perish." 17 So Mordecai went away and did exactly as Esther had commanded him.

Esther Plans a Banquet (Chapter 5)

On the third day [of the fast] Esther put on her royal robes and stood in the inner court of the king's palace opposite his [throne] room. The king was sitting on his royal throne, facing the [main] entrance of the palace. 2 When the king saw Esther the queen standing in the court, she found favor in his sight; and the king extended to her the golden scepter which was in his hand. So Esther approached and touched the top of the scepter. 3 Then the king said to her, "What is *troubling* you, Queen Esther? What is your request? It shall be given to you, up to half of the kingdom." 4 Esther said, "If it pleases the king, may the king and Haman come this day to the banquet that I have prepared for him."

5 Then the king said, "Bring Haman quickly so that we may do as Esther says." So the king and Haman came to the banquet which Esther had prepared. 6 As they drank their wine at the banquet, the king said to Esther, "What is your petition? It shall be granted to you. And what is your request? Even to half of the kingdom it shall be done." 7 Then Esther replied, "My petition and my request is this: 8 if I have found favor in the sight of the king, and if it pleases the king to grant my petition and to do as I request, may the king and Haman come to the banquet that I will prepare for them; and tomorrow I will do as the king says [and express my request]."

Haman's Pride

9 Haman went away that day joyful and in good spirits. But when he saw Mordecai at the king's gate refusing to stand up or show fear before him, he was filled with rage toward Mordecai. 10 Nevertheless, Haman controlled himself and went home. There he sent for his friends and his wife Zeresh. 11 Then Haman recounted to them the glory of his riches, the large number of his sons, and every *instance* in which the king had magnified him and how he had promoted him over the officials and servants of the king. 12 Haman also said, "Even Queen Esther let no one but me come with the king to the banquet she had prepared; and tomorrow also I am invited by her [together] with the king. 13 Yet all of this does not satisfy me as long as I see Mordecai the Jew sitting at the king's gate." 14 Then his wife Zeresh and all his friends said to him "Have a gallows fifty cubits high made, and in the morning ask the king to have Mordecai hanged on it; then go joyfully to the banquet

with the king." And the advice pleased Haman, so he had the gallows made.

The King Plans to Honor Mordecai (Chapter 6)

On that night the king could not sleep; so he ordered that the book of records *and* memorable deeds, the chronicles, be brought, and they were read before the king. 2 It was found written there how Mordecai had reported that Bigthana and Teresh, two of the king's eunuchs who were doorkeepers, had planned to attack King Ahasuerus (Xerxes). 3 The king said, "What honor or distinction has been given Mordecai for this?" Then the king's servants who attended him said, "Nothing has been done for him." 4 So the king said, "Who is in the court?" Now Haman had just entered the outer court of the king's palace to ask the king about hanging Mordecai on the gallows which he had prepared for him. 5 The king's servants said to him, "Look, Haman is standing in the court." And the king said, "Let him come in." 6 So Haman came in and the king said to him, "What is to be done for the man whom the king desires to honor?" Now Haman thought to himself, "Whom would the king desire to honor more than me?" 7 So Haman said to the king, "For the man whom the king desires to honor, 8 let a royal robe be brought which the king has worn, and the horse on which the king has ridden, and on whose head a royal crown has been placed; 9 and let the robe and the horse be handed over to one of the king's most noble officials. Let him dress the man whom the king delights to honor [in the royal robe] and lead him on horseback through the open square of the city, and proclaim before him, 'This is what shall be done for the man whom the king desires to honor.'"

Haman Must Honor Mordecai

[10] Then the king said to Haman, "Quickly take the royal robe and the horse, as you have said, and do this for Mordecai the Jew, who is sitting at the king's gate. Leave out nothing of all that you have said." [11] So Haman took the royal robe and the horse and dressed Mordecai, and led him *on horseback* through the open square of the city, proclaiming before him, "This is what shall be done for the man whom the king desires to honor."

[12] Then Mordecai returned to the king's gate. But Haman hurried to his [own] house, mourning and with his head covered [in sorrow]. [13] Then Haman told Zeresh his wife and all his friends' everything that had happened to him. Then his wise counselors and his wife Zeresh said to him, "If Mordecai, before whom you have be- gun to fall *in status*, is of Jewish heritage, you will not overcome him, but will certainly fall before him."

[14] While they were still speaking with him, the king's eunuchs (attendants) arrived and hurriedly brought Haman to the banquet which Esther had prepared.

Esther's Plea (Chapter 7)

So the king and Haman came to drink *wine* with Esther the queen. [2] And the king said to Esther on the second day also as they drank their wine, "What is your petition, Queen Esther? It shall be granted to you. And what is your request? Even to half of the kingdom, it shall be done." [3] Then Queen Esther replied, "If I have found favor in your sight, O king, and if it pleases the king, let my life be spared as my petition, and my people [be spared] as my re- quest; [4] for we have been sold, I and my people, to be destroyed, killed and wiped out of existence. Now if we had only been sold as slaves, men and women, I would have remained silent, for our hardship would not be sufficient to burden the king [by even mentioning it]." [5] Then

King Ahasuerus (Xerxes) asked Queen Esther, "Who is he, and where he, who dares to is do such a thing?" 6 Esther said, "An adversary and an enemy is Haman, this evil man." Then Haman became terrified before the king and queen.

Haman Is Hanged

7 Then in his fury, the king stood up from drinking wine *and went* into the palace garden [to decide what he should do]; but Haman stayed to plead for his life from Queen Esther, for he saw that harm had been determined against him by the king. 8 When the king returned from the palace garden to the place where they were drinking wine, Haman was falling on the couch where Esther was. Then the king said, "Will he even *attempt to* assault the queen with me in the pal- ace?" As the king spoke those words, the servants covered Haman's face [in preparation for execution]. 9 Then Harbonah, one of the eunuchs serving the king said, "Now look, there are gallows fifty cubits (75 ft.) high standing at Haman's house, which Haman made for Mordecai, whose good warning saved the king." And the king said, "Hang him on it." 10 So they hanged Haman on the gallows that he had prepared for Mordecai. Then the king's anger subsided.

Mordecai Promoted (Chapter 8)

On that day King Ahasuerus (Xerxes) gave the house of Haman, the enemy of the Jews, to Queen Esther; and Mordecai came before the king, because Esther had disclosed what [relation] he was to her. 2 The king took off his signet ring which he had taken away from Haman, and gave it to Mordecai. And Esther put Mordecai in charge of the house of Haman.

3 Then Esther spoke again to the king and fell down at his feet and wept and implored him to avert the evil *plot* of Haman the Agagite and his plan which he had devised against the Jews [because the decree to annihilate the Jews was still in effect]. 4 Then the king held out to Esther the golden scepter. So Esther arose and stood before the king. 5 Then she said, "If it pleases the king and if I have found favor before him and the matter is proper in the king's view and I am pleasing in his sight, let it be written to revoke the letters devised by Haman the son of Hammedatha, the Agagite, which he wrote [in order] to destroy the Jews who are in all the king's provinces. 6 For how can I endure to see the tragedy that will happen to my people? Or how can I endure to see the destruction of my kindred?" 7 Then King Ahasuerus said to Queen Esther and to Mordecai the Jew, "Behold, I have given Esther the house of Haman, and they have hanged him on the gallows because he stretched out his hand against the Jews.

The King's Decree Avenges the Jews

8 Also, concerning the Jews, write as you see fit, in the king's name, and seal it with the king's signet ring—for a decree which is written in the king's name and sealed with the king's signet ring may not be revoked."

9 So the king's scribes were called at that time in the third month (that is, the month of Sivan) on the twenty-third day; and it was written in accordance with everything that Mordecai commanded, to the Jews, to the chief rulers (satraps), and the governors and officials of the provinces which *extended* from India to Ethiopia (Cush), 127 provinces, to every province in its own script (writing), and to every people in their own language and to the Jews according to their script and their language. 10 He wrote [a decree] in the name

of King Ahasuerus, and sealed it with the king's ring, and sent letters by couriers on horseback, riding on the royal [mail] relay horses, the offspring of the racing mares. ¹¹ In it the king granted the Jews who were in every city *the right* to assemble and to defend their lives; to destroy, to kill, and to annihilate any armed force that might at- tack them, their little children, and women; and to take the enemies' goods as plunder, ¹² on one day in all the provinces of King Ahasuerus, the thirteenth [day] of the twelfth month (that is, the month of Adar). ¹³ A copy of the edict was to be issued as a law in every province and as a proclamation to all peoples, so that the Jews would be ready on that day, to avenge themselves on their enemies. ¹⁴ So the couriers, who were mounted on the royal relay horses, left quickly, urged on by the king's command; and the decree was issued at the citadel in Susa [the capital].

¹⁵ Then Mordecai departed from the presence of the king in royal apparel of blue and white, with a large crown of gold and with a robe of fine linen and purple wool; and the city of Susa shouted and rejoiced. ¹⁶ For [at this time] the Jews had light [a dawn of new hope] and gladness and joy and honor. ¹⁷ In each and every province and in each and every city, wherever the king's command and his decree arrived, the Jews *celebrated with* gladness and joy, a feast and a holiday. And many among the peoples of the land became Jews, for the fear of the Jews [and their God] had fallen on them.

The Jews Destroy Their Enemies (Chapter 9)

Now in the twelfth month (that is, the month of Adar) on the thirteenth day when the king's command and edict were about to be executed, on the [very] day when the enemies of the Jews had hoped to gain power over them [and slaughter them], it happened the other way around so that the Jews themselves gained power over those who hated them. 2 The Jews assembled in their cities throughout the provinces of King Ahasuerus (Xerxes) to apprehend those who wanted to do them harm; and no one could stand before them, for the fear of them [and their God] had fallen on all the peoples. 3 Even all the officials of the provinces and the chief rulers (satraps) and the governors and those who attended to the king's business supported the Jews [in defeating their enemies], because the fear of Mordecai [and his God's power] had fallen on them. 4 For Mordecai was great *and* respected in the king's palace and his fame spread throughout all the provinces; for the man Mordecai became greater and greater. 5 So the Jews struck all their enemies with the sword, killing and destroying them; and they did what they pleased to those who hated them. 6 At the citadel in Susa the Jews killed and destroyed five hundred men, 7 and [they killed] Parshandatha, Dalphon, Aspatha, 8 Poratha, Adalia, Aridatha, 9 Parmashta, Arisai, Aridai, and Vaizatha, 10 the ten sons of Haman the son of Hammedatha, the Jews' enemy; but they did not lay their hands on the plunder.

11 On that day the number of those who were killed at the citadel in Susa was reported to the king. 12 The king said to Queen Esther, "The Jews have killed and destroyed five hundred men and the ten sons of Haman at the citadel in Susa. What then have they done in the rest of the king's provinces! Now what is your petition? It shall be granted to you. What is your further request? It shall also be done." 13 Esther replied, "If it pleases the king, let it be granted to the Jews who are in Susa to act tomorrow also in accordance with the decree of today; and let [the dead bodies of] Haman's ten sons be hanged on the gallows." 14 So the king commanded it to be done; the decree was given in Susa, and they hanged [the bodies of] Haman's ten sons. 15 The Jews who were in Susa also gathered together on the fourteenth day of the month of Adar and killed

three hundred men in Susa, but they did not lay their hands on the plunder.

¹⁶ Now the rest of the Jews who were in the king's provinces assembled, to defend their lives and rid themselves of their enemies, and kill 75,000 of those who hated them; but they did not lay their hands on the plunder. ¹⁷ *This was done* on the thirteenth day of the month of Adar, and on the fourteenth day they rested and made it a day of feasting and rejoicing.

¹⁸ But the Jews who were in Susa assembled on the thirteenth and on the fourteenth of the same month, and on the fifteenth day they rested and made it a day of feasting and rejoicing. ¹⁹ Therefore the Jews of the villages, who live in the rural [unwalled] towns, make the fourteenth day of the month of Adar a holiday for rejoicing and feasting and sending choice portions *of food* to one another.

The Feast of Purim Instituted

²⁰ Now Mordecai recorded these events, and he sent letters to all the Jews who lived in all the provinces of King Ahasuerus, both near and far, ²¹ obliging them to celebrate the fourteenth day of the month of Adar, and the fifteenth day of the same month, annually, ²² because on those days the Jews rid themselves of their enemies, and as the month which was turned for them from grief to joy and from mourning into a holiday; that they should make them days of feasting and rejoicing and sending choice portions *of food* to one another and gifts to the poor.

²³ So the Jews undertook what they had started to do, and what Mordecai had written to them. ²⁴ For Haman the son of Hammedatha, the Agagite, the enemy of all the Jews, had plotted against the Jews to destroy them and had cast Pur, that is, the lot, [to find the right time] to disturb and destroy them. ²⁵ But when it came before the king, he commanded in writing that Haman's wicked

scheme which he had devised against the Jews was to return on his own head, and that he and his sons should [endure what he planned for the Jews and] be hanged on the gallows. [26] Therefore they called these days Purim after the name Pur (lot). And because of all the instructions in this letter, and what they had faced in this regard and what had happened to them, [27] the Jews established and made it a custom for themselves and for their descendants and for all who joined them, so that they would not fail to celebrate these two days as it was written and at the appointed time annually. [28] So these days were to be remembered and celebrated throughout every generation, every family, every province and every city; and these days of Purim were not to cease from among the Jews, nor their memory fade from their descendants.

[29] Then Queen Esther, the daughter of Abihail, with Mordecai the Jew, wrote with full power *and* authority to confirm this second letter about Purim. [30] He sent letters to all the Jews, to the 127 provinces of the kingdom of Ahasuerus, in words of peace and truth, [31] to establish these days of Purim [to be observed] at their appointed times, just as Mordecai the Jew and Queen Esther had established for them, and as they had established for themselves and for their descendants with instructions regarding their times of fasting and their lamentations (expressions of needing help). [32] The command of Esther established these customs for Purim, and it was written in the book [of the royal archives].

Mordecai's Greatness (Chapter 10)

King Ahasuerus (Xerxes) imposed a tax on the land and on the coastlands of the sea. [2] And all the accomplishments of his authority and strength, and the full account of the greatness of Mordecai to which the king had raised him, are they not written in the Book of the Chronicles of the Kings of Media and Persia? ³ For Mordecai the Jew was second only to King Ahasuerus, and great among the Jews and in favor with his many fellow people, for he worked for the good of his people and spoke for the welfare *and* peace of his whole nation.

Notes

Other Works by the Author

Autobiography about Dr. Sharon's life up to 2013: $16.00

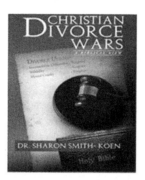

Self-help Christian book: $12.00

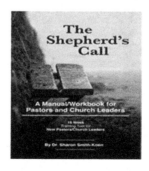

Manual for new pastors and church leaders: $16.00

Devotional for Women
$20.00

Devotional for new believers
$20.00

Women's Christian Magazine
$5.00

All Publications may be purchased via

www.inspiredwholenesscounseling.com

or

Directly from Dr. Sharon

56095435R00104

Made in the USA
Columbia, SC
20 April 2019